A Very Bright Future —Copyright ©2025 by Tony Tice
Published by UNITED HOUSE Publishing

All rights reserved. No portion of this book may be reproduced or shared in any form–electronic, printed, photocopied, recording, or by any information storage and retrieval system, without prior written permission from the publisher. The use of short quotations is permitted.

The Holy Bible, English Standard Version. ESV® Text Edition: 2016. Copyright © 2001 by Crossway Bibles, a publishing ministry of Good News Publishers.

ISBN: 978-1-952840-78-4

UNITED HOUSE Publishing
Waterford, Michigan
info@unitedhousepublishing.com
www.unitedhousepublishing.com

Cover Layout and Interior Design:
Matt Russell, In The Light Creative, matt@inthelightcreative.com

Printed in the United States of America
2025—First Edition

SPECIAL SALES
Most UNITED HOUSE books are available at special quantity discounts when purchased in bulk by corporations, organizations, and special-interest groups. For information, please e-mail orders@unitedhousepublishing.com

A VERY BRIGHT FUTURE

BOOK OF REVELATION DEVOTIONAL

TONY TICE

Table of Contents

DAY 1 - **"What Makes Heaven, Heaven"** 9
DAY 2 - **"The Sad Tale Of The Prince of Grenada"** 11
DAY 3 - **"The Good News About Sin"** 13
DAY 4 - **"The Prince And The Pauper"** 15
DAY 5 - **"Here Comes The Judge"** 17
DAY 6 - **"Misery Loves Company"** 21
DAY 7 - **"Guess Who Prays For You?"** 25
DAY 8 - **"Jesus In 3-D"** 29
DAY 9 - **"Fearful But Not Afraid"** 33
DAY 10 - **"You Can Lead A Horse . . . "** 37
DAY 11 - **"First Love"** 39
DAY 12 - **"Tried And Tested"** 43
DAY 13 - **"What Do You Think About God?"** 47
DAY 14 - **"The Most Popular Verse In The World"** 51
DAY 15 - **"Rewards That Can't Be Destroyed"** 55
DAY 16 - **"Alive But Dead"** 59
DAY 17 - **"Short But Scrappy"** 63
DAY 18 - **"Spoiled Brats"** 67
DAY 19 - **"Puny Posers"** 71
DAY 20 - **"Firm Foundation"** 75
DAY 21 - **"The Throne"** 79
DAY 22 - **"Brilliant And Beautiful"** 83
DAY 23 - **"A Beautiful Trembling"** 87
DAY 24 - **"Mind The Gap"** 89
DAY 25 - **"Unfading Glory"** 91
DAY 26 - **"Tears In Heaven"** 95

DAY 27 - **"To The Victor Go The Spoils"** 97
DAY 28 - **"Not Wasted"** 99
DAY 29 - **"Jesus > Angels"** 101
DAY 30 - **"Cape Of Good Hope"** 103
DAY 31 - **"The Four Horsemen"** 105
DAY 32 - **"Rags To Riches"** 109
DAY 33 - **Slain For The Word"** 113
DAY 34 - **"The Earth Will Quake"** 117
DAY 35 - **"A Frightening Being To Behold"** 121
DAY 36 - **"Sealed"** 125
DAY 37 - **"Israel"** 129
DAY 38 - **"The Unreached Reached"** 133
DAY 39 - **"Mercy Amidst Judgment"** 137
DAY 40 - **"Cannonballs In the Sky?"** 141
DAY 41 - **"Bowl Of Prayers"** 143
DAY 42 - **"Eagle Cry"** 145
DAY 43 - **"Spooky Creatures"** 149
DAY 44 - **"Death"** 153
DAY 45 - **"A Change Of Fortunes"** 157
DAY 46 - **"Fighting Angels"** 161
DAY 47 - **"Seafood Diet"** 165
DAY 48 - **"The Power Of A Life Lived Well"** 169
DAY 49 - **"Comeback Story"** 173
DAY 50 - **"The Ark Of The Covenant"** 177
DAY 51 - **"Satan Is A Loser"** 181
DAY 52 - **"Thrown Out"** 185
DAY 53 - **"Good News/Bad News"** 189
DAY 54 - **"Endurance Race"** 193
DAY 55 - **"Diabolical Duo"** 197
DAY 56 - **"A Heavenly Choice"** 201
DAY 57 - **"Sickle"** 205

DAY 58 - **"Worship Is A Way Of Life"**................209
DAY 59 - **"Here Comes The Judge"**..................213
DAY 60 - **"The War Already Won"**...................217
DAY 61 - **"The Man Who Fell Into A Hole"**..........221
DAY 62 - **"Conquering Lamb"**.......................225
DAY 63 - **"A Trip To The Woodshed"**................229
DAY 64 - **"Money Won't Matter"**....................233
DAY 65 - **"Blood For Blood"**.......................235
DAY 66 - **"Heavenly Worship"**......................239
DAY 67 - **"Best Wedding Ever"**.....................243
DAY 68 - **"The Tale Of Two White Horses"**..........247
DAY 69 - **"Two Roads"**.............................249
DAY 70 - **"Bullies"**...............................251
DAY 71 - **"Satan's Pit"**...........................253
DAY 72 - **"House Of Cards"**........................255
DAY 73 - **"The End"**...............................257
DAY 74 - **"Book Of Life"**..........................259
DAY 75 - **"Over Our Dead Bodies"**..................261
DAY 76 - **"The Prince"**............................265
DAY 77 - **"New"**...................................269
DAY 78 - **"Ranch Names"**...........................271
DAY 79 - **"The Coolest City"**......................273
DAY 80 - **"Evel Knievel"**..........................277
DAY 81 - **"Redo"**..................................279
DAY 82 - **"Hearing Vs. Heeding"**...................281
DAY 83 - **"Washed"**................................283
DAY 84 - **"Come"**..................................287
DAY 85 - **"Yearning For Home"**.....................289
Notes..293
About the Author.................................299

DAY 1

"What Makes Heaven, Heaven"
Revelation 1:1-2

St. Patrick lived in the 5th century. When he was sixteen, he was captured by Irish pirates from his home in Britain and taken as a slave to Ireland to look after pigs. Though Patrick had grown up in a Christian home, he never really had a relationship with God, until his captivity when he surrendered his life to Jesus. After six years in captivity, he was able to escape back home to Britain.

However, God worked in his heart; he not only forgave his captors, but he also went back to Ireland to preach the gospel to them. And that's how Christianity began to spread throughout Ireland. Patrick was a man who fell in love with Jesus, and this famous prayer of his reflects the centrality of Christ in his life:

Christ with me, Christ before me, Christ behind me,
Christ in me, Christ beneath me, Christ above me,
Christ on my right, Christ on my left,
Christ when I lie down, Christ when I sit down,
Christ in the heart of everyone who thinks of me,
Christ in the mouth of everyone who speaks of me,
Christ in the eye that sees me,
Christ in the ear that hears me.[1]

How desperately I want that prayer as a reflection of my own life. Is it a prayer for your life as well? So often, we think of Revelation as a book about the End Times. Of course, there is a lot about that in the book. But ultimately, Revelation is about who Jesus is. The opening verses make that clear.

Revelation 1:1-2 says, *"The revelation of Jesus Christ, which God gave him to show to his servants the things that must soon take place. He made it known by sending his angel to his servant John, who bore witness to the word of God and to the testimony of Jesus Christ, even to all that he saw."*

Revelation reveals to us who Jesus is, and in just the first eight verses, we learn a lot about Jesus. Throughout this journey through Revelation, I hope you don't just learn about the people, places, and events that lie ahead. I hope you leave our time in the book with a greater understanding of who the Person of Jesus really is.

Do you know what makes Heaven, Heaven? It's the Person, not the place. If we love Jesus now, though imperfectly due to the sin nature, imagine what it will be like in glory when we see Him face-to-face, without any sin in our lives. What makes Heaven, Heaven, is Jesus.

Closing Benediction: "May the Holy Spirit reveal the excellency of Jesus Christ to us in a fresh and impactful way as we study the holy book of Revelation. Amen."

DAY 2

"The Sad Tale Of The Prince of Grenada"

Revelation 1:3

I came across a story years ago that was first published in Psychology Today, and it has always stuck with me. It was a story about the Prince of Grenada, who was an heir to the Spanish crown.[2] He had been sentenced to life in solitary confinement in a Madrid prison, also called "The Place of the Skull."

The prince was given one book to read the entire time: the Bible. With only one book to read, he read it hundreds and hundreds of times. The prince died in his prison cell after thirty-three years of confinement. When they came to clean out his cell, they discovered notes written on the wall with his nails. They were notes about the Bible.

For instance, he wrote that Psalm 118:8 was the middle verse of the Bible. And that Ezra 7:21 contains all the letters of the alphabet except the letter "j." He jotted down that the ninth verse of the eighth chapter of Esther is the longest verse in the Bible. He also noted that no word or name more than six syllables can be found in the Bible.

What makes this story both memorable and sad is that this individual spent over thirty years of his life studying the Word of God, night and day, yet it appeared that he had never made any religious or spiritual commitment to Christ. He simply became an expert at Bible trivia.

We have been given the Bible for transformation not just information. In Revelation 1:3, we are reminded of this: *"Blessed is the one who reads aloud the words of this prophecy, and blessed are those who hear, and who keep what is written in it, for the time is near."*

Reading and listening to the Bible is hugely important. But the end of the verse says we are to "keep" what is written. That means we are to apply it to our daily lives. John, the author, gives two reasons why.

First, we will be "blessed." And secondly, "for the time is near." This means Christ could come back at any moment. You want God to pour out His blessings on your life? Do you want to hear those words from Jesus, "Well done, good and faithful servant?" Read, listen, and apply God's Word to your life. We can let God's Word transform our lives, or we can just be really good at Bible trivia. What will you do with God's Word this week?

Closing Benediction: "May the Word of God refresh our souls this week. May the Holy Spirit guide us in how to apply it to our lives in a way that makes us look more and more like Jesus. Amen."

DAY 3

"The Good News About Sin"

Revelation 1:4-5a

John Phillips told the following story in his commentary *Exploring Romans*. A self-righteous man once boasted to his Christian friend, "You know, John, I'm not such a bad fellow. There are many worse than I!" His friend replied, "Ivor, you are measuring yourself by the wrong standard. You measure yourself by the harlots and drunkards you see on Skid Row and you feel quite satisfied by comparison. But go and measure yourself alongside Jesus Christ and see how you make out."[3] No person's life cuts much of a figure when placed alongside the perfect life of Christ. The life of the Lord Jesus shows us how crooked and defiled our own lives really are. It is no wonder God says in Romans 3:10: "None is righteous, no, not one." The truth about us that this story depicts would be depressing if it weren't for one significant thing . . . the gospel!

The gospel changes everything. The gospel allows us to have a relationship with a perfect God despite our sinful nature. The gospel means that one day, we can spend all eternity with Him. This is the message of Revelation. Jesus will return and defeat all evil, and establish His eternal kingdom.

In the opening chapter of Revelation, we have a description of Jesus that reveals the heart of the gospel. Revelation 1:4-5a reads, *"John to the seven churches that are in Asia: Grace to you and peace from him who is and who was and who is to come, and from the seven spirits who are before his throne, and from Jesus Christ, the faithful witness, the firstborn of the dead, and the ruler of kings on earth."*

While all three Persons of the Trinity are mentioned in these verses, the focus is clearly on Jesus. It says He is the "faithful witness." The Greek word for "witness" is where we get our English word martyr. A martyr is one who dies for a cause. Jesus was committed to a cause —the redemption of mankind. He was faithful, all the way to the cross to pay for our sins.

Jesus is the "firstborn of the dead." This means all who come after Him can be raised to glory, because Christ defeated the grave. And Jesus is "the ruler of kings on earth." Jesus may have come as a suffering servant, but He will return someday as the King of kings. Every knee will bow on that day.

These three descriptions are the heart of the glorious gospel. He died. He rose. And He will return again. We are sinners, but Jesus is our Savior. Come let us worship the King!

Closing Benediction: "May the reality of the gospel bring us great joy and hope today. May the Lord open a door for us to share this glorious gospel with people who need it. Amen."

DAY 4

"The Prince And The Pauper"
Revelation 1:5b-6

In 1882, Mark Twain wrote the novel *The Prince and the Pauper*. It tells the story of two boys, born on the same day, who look identical. One of the boys, Tom Canty, is a pauper who lives with an abusive, alcoholic father in a poor section of London. The other boy is Prince Edward, son of King Henry VIII. The boys end up meeting each other and decide to switch places temporarily. Much of the book is on the lessons each of them learns in seeing how the other lives.

When they switch back to their real identities, each is changed by the experience. When King Henry VIII dies, Edward becomes king and rules compassionately, having lived among the poor and hurting. Tom is made the "King's Ward," having a place in the royal family for the rest of his life.

The Prince and the Pauper, in some ways, portrays the gospel of Jesus Christ. Jesus, as Son of God, left the glories of the heavenly palace to live among a spiritually poor and helpless people. And He did something about our spiritual poverty. He died on the cross. When He rose from the dead, He returned to Heaven and is seated at the right hand of God.

And what about us? What did it do for us to have the "Prince" become the "Pauper" to then return to the throne? Today's verses from Revelation 1:5b-6 tell us, *"To him who loves us and has freed us from our sins by his blood and made us a kingdom, priests to his God and Father, to him be glory and dominion forever and ever. Amen."*

These verses tell us three things: Jesus loves us, His death (and resurrection) freed us from the penalty of sin, and we are now part of God's Kingdom, with the role of priesthood. This is the "Great Exchange"—from pauper to prince (and princess, for the ladies).

So, how should we respond to this great exchange? Well, we give gratitude through praise and worship. We can also show our thankfulness in how we live. We live as "priests of His Kingdom." A priest, in Bible times, spoke to God on behalf of the people and spoke to people on behalf of God.

Are we living out the role God has given us? Do we daily offer sacrifices of praise? Do we serve those around us? Are we going to God in prayer on behalf of the people? Are we going to people, sharing the gospel and discipling them, on behalf of God? It's the only proper response to God's glorious grace.

Closing Benediction: "May God use us today in our priestly roles. May God bring someone into our lives to serve. May the reality of God's great exchange cause us to offer up passionate sacrifices of praise. Amen."

DAY 5

"Here Comes The Judge"
Revelation 1:7-8

On December 28, 1908, an earthquake destroyed the city of Messina, Sicily. 84,000 people were killed in the quake. According to John Lawrence, in his book *Down to Earth*, Messina was a wicked and irreligious town. The book says a newspaper in Messina printed a parody against God three days earlier on Christmas Day.[4]

Was this an example of God's judgment on ungodly people who mocked His name? I have no idea. Honestly, I have not been able to validate the claim. But I do know this: God has every right to judge people for their sin and dish out whatever discipline He sees fit. We live in a society that doesn't think we should judge others. Live and let live. This mindset extends to God. We like the idea of a benevolent and merciful God, but a God who may choose to deliver harsh punishment? That makes us unsettled.

The reality is we don't have the right to create a version of God we like or a God who may be more accepting of our culture. God is who He is. Yes, He is a benevolent and merciful God, but He still is holy and just. God will deal with sin, and He has every right to. And while the return of Christ and the establishment of His eternal Kingdom will be amazing for those who know Him, it is a time of intense wrath for those who have refused to receive Him as Lord and Savior.

I believe there will be a seven-year Tribulation, literally "hell on earth." Sin will be punished. People interpret the End Times differently, but I believe Christians will be raptured to heaven before the Tribulation. After the seven years, Christ will return to establish His Kingdom. This is known as the Second Coming of Christ. I believe that is the description we are given in Revelation 1:7-8:

"Behold, he is coming with the clouds, and every eye will see him, even those who pierced him, and all tribes of the earth will wail on account of him. Even so. Amen. 'I am the Alpha and the Omega,' says the Lord God, 'who is and who was and who is to come, the Almighty.'"

God is "Almighty," meaning there is no one even close to His mightiness. He's the "Alpha" (first letter of the Greek alphabet) and the "Omega" (last letter of the Greek alphabet). He's the beginning and the end. Every life will give an account. For us believers, His coming is a time for rejoicing, but for those who are not, it is a time of wailing.

So what do we do with this reality? We live daily in humble adoration for what we will be spared from. When life doesn't seem fair, when it seems like the bad guys are winning, we stop and remember that God will right all wrongs. And, when we think about the coming judgment, may our hearts break for the people we know who don't know Jesus. May it fuel us to share the gospel with them and to pray for their salvation.

Closing Benediction: "May the reality of God's judgment humble us and yet produce great gratitude within us, because we are spared from His wrath. May we pray for the lost and share Jesus with them. Amen."

DAY 6

"Misery Loves Company"
Revelation 1:9-11

Misery loves company. I always thought the meaning behind that well-known phrase was that if a person feels miserable, it helps to be with others who can identify with their pain. But I did a little research on the phrase.

Apparently "misery loves company" dates all the way back to the 16th century from a play called *Dr. Faustus*. It's a play about a miserable man who signs a pact with the devil to live twenty-four more years. The famous phrase comes from the lips of one of Satan's demons in reply to a question about why Satan was seeking to enlarge his kingdom.

In other words, extending twenty-four more years to the man meant sharing his misery with others who, as a result, may experience more misery themselves. So, the original idea of the phrase is that a miserable person finds company in other miserable people.

I don't know about you, but that sounds really depressing: finding other miserable people to be miserable with. Let me try to sanctify the phrase for us. Let's understand "misery loves company" from a Biblical perspective—the idea of sharing in each other's suffering.

There is something about being with people who can relate to our pain but not so that we can remain in the pain. Sharing in each other's suffering should bring empathy and lead to comfort for each other. It should lead to praying for each other and remembering to encourage one another.

In Revelation 1:9-11, John talks about sharing in the same suffering the recipients of his letter were experiencing: *"I, John, your brother and partner in the tribulation and the kingdom and the patient endurance that are in Jesus, was on the island called Patmos on account of the word of God and the testimony of Jesus. I was in the Spirit on the Lord's day, and I heard behind me a loud voice like a trumpet saying, "Write what you see in a book and send it to the seven churches, to Ephesus and to Smyrna and to Pergamum and to Thyatira and to Sardis and to Philadelphia and to Laodicea."*

As we will learn in chapters two and three of Revelation, these seven churches were persecuted because of their commitment to Christ. John opens his letter by reminding them he, too, was facing persecution for his commitment to Christ and the Word of God. He was imprisoned on an island and treated harshly, as an old man, probably in his nineties. And he had a message from the Savior, who Himself experienced suffering on earth. While Revelation is a prophecy of coming events, it is first and foremost a book about Christ and the comfort we can find in Him, and a comfort that rests in the future hope of glory.

Until that future day of glory, find daily strength in the Savior and find it in a body of believers from which you can draw strength. Have a mentor, an accountability partner, or just an encourager you can hang out with. And always remind each other that the Suffering Servant will one day return as a Conquering King. Misery loves company, not to feel better that others are hurting, but so the hurting can find comfort in Christ.

Closing Benediction: "May the God of all comfort bring comfort to our hearts and minds today. May we find others to share our suffering with so that we might find hope and encouragement for today. May the reality of the return of Jesus fill us with joy. Amen."

DAY 7

"Guess Who Prays For You?"
Revelation 1:12-13

It is easy for us to think that the stars of the church are the pastors who preach God's Word or the worship leaders who can sing with beautiful voices and help lead us to the throne of God in worship. These are important roles in the life of the church body, but in reality, there are no stars but one, and that's the Lord Jesus Christ; however, we tend to think of certain positions and functions in the church as more valuable than others.

In 1 Corinthians 12:22, Paul says that "the parts of the body that seem to be weaker are indispensable." I often think about the day when believers will stand before the Judgment Seat of Christ, which is discussed in 1 Corinthians 3 and 2 Corinthians 5. I can't help but think that we might be surprised at who receives many crowns and who may not receive as many as we thought they would.

You know who I think are the unsung heroes in the church? The ones that we might be surprised at their degree of impact when we "receive what is due," as 2 Corinthians 5:10 puts it. It's the moms who are tenacious prayer warriors for their families and for other people in their lives.

Pastor and author Charles Swindoll once said, "As far back as

I can remember, my mother would have me down by the bed at night with her, praying. I can still hear her voice calling my name to God and telling him that she wanted me to follow him in whatever he called me to do."[5]

The prayers of our mothers are important, but there is someone even more important who prays for us. Today's passage gives us a picture of who it is. Let's look at Revelation 1:12-13: *"Then I turned to see the voice that was speaking to me, and on turning I saw seven golden lampstands, and in the midst of the lampstands one like a son of man, clothed with a long robe and with a golden sash around his chest."*

This vision is clearly a description of Jesus. While this vision of Jesus is not literally what the post-resurrected Savior looks like, it is meant to symbolize who Jesus is. And in verse 13, the vision of Jesus "clothed with a long robe and with a golden sash" is a clear depiction of Jesus as our High Priest. Exodus 39 says that these were the garments the high priest wore at the Temple. Jesus is our High Priest.

That means He goes to God the Father on our behalf and prays for us. Think about that—Jesus prays for you! Hebrews 2:18 says Jesus is "a merciful and faithful high priest." Because of that, Hebrews 4:16 says we can "with confidence draw near to the throne of grace." Come confidently, boldly, and humbly to God's throne of grace. Jesus is praying for you.

Closing Benediction: "May we pray with a renewed sense of boldness, knowing our Savior intercedes on our behalf. May we find comfort and courage knowing we have the ultimate defender, Jesus Christ, the Son of Man, the Son of God. Amen."

DAY 8

"Jesus In 3-D"

Revelation 1:14-16

Do you remember the Magic Eye pictures that were popular in the 1990s? They were these 3-D pictures that would appear within a kaleidoscopic image, if you looked just right at them.

They were so popular that they published a collection of the images in a book, which remained on the *New York Times* best-seller list for over seventy weeks. The key to seeing the 3-D image was learning to see behind all of the seemingly random dots. It could take a while to train the eyes to do this, but once you did, you could see the image emerge.

If we are careful in our study of God's Word, we can see the true image of Jesus emerge for us, not the cultural depiction of Jesus, who, oftentimes, is a very European-looking white man with blonde hair and blue eyes; who I would suggest is somewhat effeminate looking; a hippie-like figure who wants us "to make love, not war."

This, of course, is not an accurate view of Jesus. Though He is very much loving, He is much more than we often picture Him. The vision given to John of Jesus helps the real Jesus emerge. Look at Revelation 1:14-16:

> *The hairs of his head were white, like white wool, like snow. His eyes were like a flame of fire, his feet were like burnished bronze, refined in a furnace, and his voice was like the roar of many waters. In his right hand he held seven stars, from his mouth came a sharp two-edged sword, and his face was like the sun shining in full strength.*

There is a lot of symbolism here, so I'm going to give a "Cliff Notes" version of them. Jesus' hair is depicted as white. White hair reflects old age and wisdom. It's similar to Daniel's vision of God in Daniel 7:9 when He is referred to as the "Ancient of Days." Jesus is eternal and all-wise.

John says, "His eyes were like a flame of fire." The idea is that His gaze instantly pierces into the deepest part of our soul. Nothing is unseen by Jesus, good or bad. Fire in the Bible is connected to judgment. Jesus will judge the living and the dead.

With feet of bronze, Jesus will trample down on all the wickedness in this world. His voice is like the roar of many waters. Jesus will bring a loud and terrifying voice to those who refuse to bow a knee to the Savior.

A sharp, two-edged sword was coming out of Jesus' mouth. As John 1 says, Jesus is the Word, and the Bible says the Word of God is like a double-edged sword. Jesus, like a sword, will divide those who follow Him and those who do not, as depicted in Revelation 19. When Jesus comes with a sword and His holy army, the wicked will be slain.

White as snow. Fiery eyes. Bronze feet. The voice of roaring waters. A sword-like mouth. And a face that shines like the sun in full strength, depicting the glory of Jesus. No, this is not hippie Jesus telling us "to make love, not war." This is a picture of the coming King who will right every wrong, establish His eternal kingdom, and reign in power and glory. This is the real Jesus. This is our King. Bow in holy worship.

Closing Benediction: "May we see clearly how glorious our Savior is. May we live in obedience to our loving and holy King. May He have complete reign in our lives. Amen."

DAY 9

"Fearful But Not Afraid"

Revelation 1:17-18

One time in college, I was playing in a pick-up basketball game, and it got a little heated. A player from the other team was talking a lot of trash, and to make matters worse, he was just a high schooler visiting his brother. As the game went on, I got more and more ticked at this high school punk, and, adding further insult to injury, that kid's team beat ours. I was pretty hot going into the locker room. As I entered, I saw the kid at his locker getting changed. I don't know what got into me (okay, it was pride), but I took the ball in my hand and threw it as his, um, "backside." I was instantly embarrassed at my lack of self-restraint.

But when he turned around, I was beyond embarrassed. It wasn't the high school punk. It was a highly esteemed seminary professor! Never one lacking in words, I was utterly speechless. I had just thrown a basketball at the bare bottom of a Biblical scholar. I never felt so ashamed and terrified in my entire life.

Have you ever been in the presence of someone who you highly respected and felt unworthy to stand before them? Especially, like me, when you had done something not very respectable? Thank goodness this man was a humble and gracious man, who actually tried to make me feel better about what had happened.

I know this example is small in comparison, but I thought of this incident after reading today's passage. Let's take a look at Revelation 1:17-18: *"When I saw him, I fell at his feet as though dead. But he laid his right hand on me, saying, "Fear not, I am the first and the last, and the living one. I died, and behold I am alive forevermore, and I have the keys of Death and Hades."*

Standing before Jesus Christ, who has eternally existed, and who has defeated the grave to ensure our salvation, and who holds in His hands the eternal fate of all mankind, John did what probably all of us would have done. He fell down in holy terror.

Jesus' perfect holiness probably made John instantly aware of his own sinfulness. It was often the case with people in the Bible who encountered a vision of God. I love the response of Jesus: "Fear not." John was a believer, so he did not have to be afraid of God.

There's a difference between a healthy fear of God and being afraid of God. Believers in Christ need not be afraid because the blood of Christ covers us. In fact, it was John who wrote in 1 John 4:18: "There is no fear in love, but perfect love casts out fear. For fear has to do with punishment, and whoever fears has not been perfected in love."

Let us have a reverential awe of Jesus. That is what the fear of the Lord means. But let us not be afraid of the Savior. His perfect love casts out fear. He lovingly shepherds His own. Draw near in love and in awe of Jesus.

Closing Benediction: "May we have a profound awe of Jesus as we draw intimately near to Him this week. May we be reminded that His love is perfect, and so, under His care, we need not fear. Amen."

DAY 10

"You Can Lead A Horse . . . "

Revelation 1:19-20

I'm sure you've heard the expression, "You can lead a horse to water, but you can't make it drink." I recently saw a cartoon of a horse near water, with a caption of the horse saying, "I'm just not thirsty, okay? Why does that bother you people so much?"

If you have walked with Christ for any length of time, you have likely experienced the frustration of trying to help someone understand the importance of reading and applying the Bible to their lives, only to have them respond with indifference. I've been a pastor for over thirty years, and that horse expression has come to mind many times.

Jesus has provided all we need for salvation and Christ-like living, but we must thirst for it. Today's passage reminds me that Jesus provides for His church, but the church must embrace His leadership for its lives.

Let's finish out chapter 1 of Revelation, verses 19-20: *"Write therefore the things that you have seen, those that are and those that are to take place after this. As for the mystery of the seven stars that you saw in my right hand, and the seven golden lampstands, the seven stars are the angels of the seven churches, and the seven lampstands are the seven churches."*

Think about this for a moment. Jesus is writing letters of instruction for seven specific churches, and it says each of these churches has angels. Now, the Greek word for angels means messengers, so it could be literal angels or human messengers. If it's literal angels, that would be pretty amazing. It could indicate that churches have guardian angels, just as each of us, as believers, possibly have. I'm not entirely sure, but I certainly love that idea.

What I do know for sure is that Jesus wants to lead and protect His churches. It's significant that the stars are in His "right hand." This represents His protection, His upholding, and guidance of the churches. But, as the saying goes, "You can lead a horse to water, but you can't make it drink." As we will see in chapters two and three, these churches weren't always thirsty for Jesus or His leadership.

How about us? Are we thirsty for Jesus? Thirsty enough to let Him have the reins of our lives? Will we submit to the Lordship of Jesus in our lives and in our churches? Because that's where protection and guidance and impact comes. Do we want to be lampstands that shine for Jesus? If so, let us thirst after Jesus.

Closing Benediction: "May our churches and may our individual lives shine brightly of the glorious goodness of our Savior. May we thirst after Jesus and drink in His daily presence. Amen."

DAY 11

"First Love"

Revelation 2:1-7

I remember a very busy season of ministry a number of years ago. We had experienced exponential growth, but I was not living at a sustainable pace. I was young and had not learned the importance of empowering others to do the ministry's work. I was arrogant and thought I had to have my hand in everything for the ministry to succeed.

One of the consequences of going too fast was neglecting my most important ministry—my family and, more specifically, my relationship with my wife, Becky. I was not taking the time to grow our relationship. I was taking her for granted. It took a while, but it finally got through my thick head. I could potentially have a successful ministry, but I would fail as a husband. I am so thankful for God's grace and my wife's grace. Neither of them gave up on me.

I made adjustments, and our relationship has flourished ever since. What adjustment did I make? I started courting my wife again. We made time to connect every night. We started having weekly date nights and decided that once a year, just the two of us would go on vacation together. I went back and behaved like I did when I first fell in love with my beautiful bride.

The passage we are looking at today reminds us that we can be busy doing good things but at the expense of the more important thing . . . love. This week, we look at the first four of seven churches Jesus had a message for, and the first one is the church in Ephesus. Let's look at Revelation 2:1-7:

> *To the angel of the church in Ephesus write: 'The words of him who holds the seven stars in his right hand, who walks among the seven golden lampstands.*
> *"'I know your works, your toil and your patient endurance, and how you cannot bear with those who are evil, but have tested those who call themselves apostles and are not, and found them to be false. I know you are enduring patiently and bearing up for my name's sake, and you have not grown weary. But I have this against you, that you have abandoned the love you had at first. Remember therefore from where you have fallen; repent, and do the works you did at first. If not, I will come to you and remove your lampstand from its place, unless you repent. Yet this you have: you hate the works of the Nicolaitans, which I also hate. He who has an ear, let him hear what the Spirit says to the churches. To the one who conquers I will grant to eat of the tree of life, which is in the paradise of God.'*

This church was serving. They were enduring. They were refusing to put up with ungodly teaching or living. I mean, they seemed like a real success. But Jesus said that they had abandoned their first love. They were going through the motions. They had stopped pursuing the love of God above all else.

Working for God can't replace loving God. We don't work for His love; our work flows out of our love for Him. As the Apostle Paul once said in 2 Corinthians 5:14, "The love of Christ compels me." Have you forsaken your first love? Are you going through the motions spiritually? If so, Jesus has given the remedy in v. 5: Remember. Repent. Redo.

Remember when you first fell in love with Jesus? If your zeal has gone away, cry out to God, repent, and ask Him to renew your love for Him. John says to then redo. Redo what? What you did when you fell in love with Jesus. Spend quality time with Him. Make it a priority to talk with Him each day. Root out the sin that hurts your relationship with Him.

It's no different from what I had to do to return to a deeper love for my wife. I needed to make her a priority, be intentional about spending time with her, and remove those things that kept me from prioritizing her. Those are the things we need to do with Jesus. Let us return to our first love.

Closing Benediction: "May we return to our first love. May the way we prioritize our daily time reveal that Jesus is first in our lives. And in doing so, may our love and zeal for the Savior abound. Amen."

DAY 12

"Tried And Tested"

Revelation 2:8-11

It's fascinating to see how different our kids are from one another. For some of our kids, sports come naturally. For others, not so much. Some of our kids love to learn and work really hard in school. Well, actually, one of the six does. They all get pretty good grades (thanks to their mother), but one of them really, really, really tries hard.

If this child got a B on a test, it would demoralize her. Growing up, I was perfectly content with the consistency of getting C's. Test day was never a good day. I would pray that the teacher would grade on the curve. The thing about tests is that they reveal how much you have learned and, oftentimes, in my case, how much more still needs to be learned. I want us to think about that today as we look at the church of Smyrna in Revelation 2. Look at verses 8-11:

And to the angel of the church in Smyrna write: 'The words of the first and the last, who died and came to life.
"'I know your tribulation and your poverty (but you are rich) and the slander of those who say that they are Jews and are not, but are a synagogue of Satan. Do not fear what you are about to suffer. Behold, the devil is about to throw some of you into prison, that you may be tested, and for ten days you

> *will have tribulation. Be faithful unto death, and I will give you the crown of life. He who has an ear, let him hear what the Spirit says to the churches. The one who conquers will not be hurt by the second death.'*

As you can see, Smyrna passed the test with Jesus. This is the only church that didn't receive a rebuke from Jesus. Maybe He didn't want to be too hard on them because of all the persecution they were facing, as they lived in an ungodly city.

As a result of their commitment to Christ, they were experiencing suffering and persecution, but notice what Jesus says: Tribulation was testing them. In 1 Peter 1:6-7, Peter writes, "In this you rejoice, though now for a little while, if necessary, you have been grieved by various trials, so that the tested genuineness of your faith—more precious than gold that perishes though it is tested by fire—may be found to result in praise and glory and honor at the revelation of Jesus Christ."

Trials and tribulations can produce a testing faith that is more precious than any riches the world offers. Preacher Vance Havner once said, "A faith that hasn't been tested, is a faith that can't be trusted."[6] I didn't like tests in school, and honestly, I don't like the tests of tribulation. But I sure love what they can produce.

Trials can deepen our dependency on God. It can make us spiritually tougher. As we learn to go through pain, it can help equip us to help others in their pain better. And there's so much more. You want a faith that can be trusted? That comes from a faith that is tested. Jesus began His address to Smyrna by reminding them that He was "the first and the last, who died and came to life." Jesus is eternal. Jesus defeated the grave. That means we have resurrection power to endure the testing of our faith through tribulations.

Closing Benediction: "May we suffer well if that's what our loving Savior has for us. May we pass the test as we keep our eyes on our resurrected Lord. Amen."

DAY 13

"What Do You Think About God?"

Revelation 2:12-17

Pew Research Center conducted a survey a few years back in which it asked Americans the question, "Do you believe in God or not?" The good news is that 80% of Americans believed in God. The bad news is that only 56% of those surveyed believed in the God of the Bible. My guess is that if the survey had explored views on God more deeply, some of the 56% would have at least some unbiblical views on God.

Fewer and fewer people are reading the Bible and, therefore, are less discerning in accurately understanding who God is. And this is a big deal. A.W. Tozer tells us why in his book *The Knowledge of the Holy*. He writes: "What comes into our minds when we think about God is the most important thing about us."[7]

In other words, our view of God affects how we understand ourselves and how we behave. Remember this: Our beliefs determine our behaviors. If I see God as a glorified "White-haired grandpa in the sky" who just wants to pamper me, then I won't take holiness very seriously, nor my sin.

To go to the other extreme, if I see God as a harsh disciplinarian, I will go through life walking on eggshells and being afraid of God instead of embracing the love of God. What we think about God is the most important thing about us, and our belief of God will impact our behavior before God. We see this in Jesus' address to the church in Pergamum. Look at verses 12-17:

And to the angel of the church in Pergamum write:
'The words of him who has the sharp two-edged sword.
"'I know where you dwell, where Satan's throne is. Yet you hold fast my name, and you did not deny my faith even in the days of Antipas, my faithful witness, who was killed among you, where Satan dwells. But I have a few things against you: you have some there who hold the teaching of Balaam, who taught Balak to put a stumbling block before the sons of Israel, so that they might eat food sacrificed to idols and practice sexual immorality. So also you have some who hold the teaching of the Nicolaitans. Therefore repent. If not, I will come to you soon and war against them with the sword of my mouth. He who has an ear, let him hear what the Spirit says to the churches. To the one who conquers, I will give some of the hidden manna, and I will give him a white stone, with a new name written on the stone that no one knows except the one who receives it.'

There's a lot here, but we'll focus on one thing. Despite being a church that held tight to God and did not deny Him in a godless culture, the church had one significant problem. Some false teachings, the teachings of Balaam and the Nicolaitans, occurred in the church.

And just like these beliefs affected the behavior of those who accepted Balaam's teaching in the Old Testament (Numbers 22), it was happening with the New Testament church of Pergamum. And guess what? It may not be Balaam or the Nicolaitans' teachings, but there is false teaching that happens in sermons, Christian books, and worship songs in today's churches as well; wrong beliefs lead to wrong behavior.

So what do we do about it? Be a passionate student of the Word of God! Prioritize daily time in God's presence to experience firsthand who God truly is. This is so important because, "What comes into our minds when we think about God is the most important thing about us."

Closing Benediction: "May we pursue wholeheartedly the real God of the Bible. May we soak up God's Word with a hunger that only God can fill, and may our beliefs impact our behavior, to the glory of God. Amen."

DAY 14

"The Most Popular Verse In The World"

Revelation 2:18-29

I grew up watching sports in the 70's and 80's. It was not uncommon to see Rollen Stewart, known as Rainbow Man, positioned in a prominent spot wearing a rainbow-colored curly wig and holding a sign that read, "John 3:16."

In those days, it was the most-known verse in the Bible. In fact, you probably know it without looking: "For God so loved the world, that he gave his only Son, that whoever believes in him should not perish but have eternal life."

It's a great verse about the gospel and still very well known, but I think another verse has become perhaps the most known and quoted, both inside and outside the church. The verse is Matthew 7:1: "Judge not, that you be not judged." I can almost guarantee someone has mentioned that verse to you at some point in your life.

But here's the problem. Most of the time, the person sharing it takes it out of the context in which Jesus said it. For most people, when they say the verse, what they're saying is that nobody has a right to judge their actions. But that's not Jesus' point in Matthew 7. He was talking about a type of judging that was hypocritical.

But you can see why people want that verse to say what they want it to say. We live in a world that places a high value on tolerance, not what the word officially means, which is respecting and not retaliating against the views of someone else.

People like the new way the word is being defined, which is needing to consider someone else's views as equally valid as yours, even if the views contradict one another. It's never speaking against another person's views or actions. And it's often the Christians buying into the new definition of tolerance.

Well, that definition is inconsistent with Scripture. We can call sin, sin. We don't have to accept everyone's views and actions as right if it feels right for them. It's okay to judge a person's actions in light of God's Word. And for brothers and sisters in Christ, we should speak the truth in love to one another. This was the issue in the church of Thyatira. Let's take a look at Revelation 2:18-29:

And to the angel of the church in Thyatira write: 'The words of the Son of God, who has eyes like a flame of fire, and whose feet are like burnished bronze. "'I know your works, your love and faith and service and patient endurance, and that your latter works exceed the first. But I have this against you, that you tolerate that woman Jezebel, who calls herself a prophetess and is teaching and seducing my servants to practice sexual immorality and to eat food sacrificed to idols.

I gave her time to repent, but she refuses to repent of her sexual immorality. Behold, I will throw her onto a sickbed, and those who commit adultery with her I will throw into great tribulation, unless they repent of her works, and I will strike her children dead. And all the churches will know that I am he who searches mind and heart, and I will give to each of you according to your works. But to the rest of you in Thyatira, who do not hold this teaching, who have not learned what some call the deep things of Satan, to you I say, I do not lay on you any other burden. Only hold fast what you have until I come. The one who conquers and who keeps my works until the end, to him I will give authority over the nations, and he will rule them with a rod of iron, as when earthen pots are broken in pieces, even as I myself have received authority from my Father. And I will give him the morning star. He who has an ear, let him hear what the Spirit says to the churches.'

A lot is going on in these verses, but I want us to focus on the weakness of this church. They refused to deal with sin. The sin of a woman nicknamed Jezebel (after the evil queen from the Old Testament). The church needs to start taking sin seriously. We have to be willing to speak the truth, even if it's unpopular in our world. We must be willing to obey Jesus by speaking the truth in love. Is there someone who needs to hear the truth in your life?

Closing Benediction: "May we have the courage and the conviction to stand up to sin around us. May we love people enough to lovingly confront them when needed. Amen."

DAY 15

"Rewards That Can't Be Destroyed"

Revelation 2:7, 10c-11, 17, 26-29

My mom has dedicated the downstairs of her house to all the awards my sisters and I have won over the years. Now, it's not a competition, but for the record, I have the most. I think I've gotten about sixty trophies over the years. I had a successful high school and college athletic career playing baseball, basketball, and soccer.

The most meaningful ones would be my college All-American trophies from soccer, and my plaque for making our college hall of fame. The oddest one would be the trophy I got in grade school for winning a city-wide bean bag competition. While looking at these trophies is a fun stroll down memory lane, the truth is, if these trophies were destroyed, I wouldn't lose a moment's sleep.

The reason is that I'm living for the rewards that can't be destroyed. I'm talking about the rewards given by the Savior. After each critique Jesus gives to the churches, He ends by giving them the hope of eternal rewards if they listen to His instructions. Let's look at what they are for the four churches covered in this chapter. Revelation 2:

> V. 7: *"To the one who conquers I will grant to eat of the tree of life, which is in the paradise of God."*
>
> Vs. 10-11: *"Be faithful unto death, and I will give you the crown of life . . . The one who conquers will not be hurt by the second death."*
>
> V. 17: *"To the one who conquers I will give some of the hidden manna, and I will give him a white stone, with a new name written on the stone that no one knows except the one who receives it.'*

Vs. 26-29: *"The one who conquers and who keeps my works until the end, to him I will give authority over the nations, and he will rule them with a rod of iron, as when earthen pots are broken in pieces, even as I myself have received authority from my Father. And I will give him the morning star."*

So if you combine them all, here are the promises of reward from Jesus: eating from the Tree of Life, receiving the crown of life, not being hurt by the second death (which is the lake of fire), receiving hidden manna, receiving a white stone with a name on it, authority over the nations, and receiving the morning star.

We aren't going to dissect each one individually, but when you look at them as a whole, it's clear that the rewards are given when we get to Heaven, which means, we should invest our lives now into the things that will lead to eternal rewards in Heaven.

Paul offers this challenge for us in I Corinthians 3:14-15: "If the work that anyone has built on the foundation survives, he will receive a reward. If anyone's work is burned up, he will suffer loss, though he himself will be saved, but only as through fire."

I don't know what exactly these rewards will look like, but one thing I know is that you don't want to be that poor person who barely escapes the flames. We should freely use our time, talents, and treasures to serve Christ and His kingdom, for the Day will reveal all we've done.

Let's make it our goal for that day of reward to be a day filled with a bounty of trophies. Though, when we see our precious Savior face to face, we will lay those treasures down at His feet. The presence of Jesus will be the only reward we'll ever need.

Closing Benediction: "May the reality of rewards in heaven fuel us to give our time, treasures, and talents to the Lord who saved us from our sins. May we pour out our lives in service to the Savior. Amen."

DAY 16

"Alive But Dead"

Revelation 3:1-6

A movie came out my senior year of high school called *Weekend at Bernie's*. It was one of those goofy movies you had to watch in the right mood. The plot was about two co-workers who were invited by their boss, Bernie, to spend the weekend at a luxury island. When they arrived at his house, they discovered he was dead.

Afraid of becoming suspects of murder and wanting to enjoy the luxurious weekend, they treated the boss like a human puppet and made people believe he was still alive. The "humor" was in the attempts of the two guys to try and make their boss appear alive, even though he was dead.

In today's passage, Jesus is writing to a church that appeared alive, yet was actually dead. Look at Revelation 3:1-6:

And to the angel of the church in Sardis write: 'The words of him who has the seven spirits of God and the seven stars. "'I know your works. You have the reputation of being alive, but you are dead. Wake up, and strengthen what remains and is about to die, for I have not found your works complete in the sight of my God. Remember, then, what you received and heard. Keep it, and repent. If you will not wake up, I will come like a thief, and you will not know at what hour I will come against you. Yet you have still a few names in Sardis, people who have not soiled their garments, and they will walk with me in white, for they are worthy. The one who conquers will be clothed thus in white garments, and I will never blot his name out of the book of life. I will confess his name before my Father and before his angels. He who has an ear, let him hear what the Spirit says to the churches.'

You can be busy for Christ but not really be alive in Christ. It was Jesus, sixty-some years earlier, who shared these sobering words about individuals who were very active in religious activity in Matthew 7:22-23: "On that day many will say to me, 'Lord, Lord, did we not prophesy in your name, and cast out demons in your name, and do many mighty works in your name?' And then will I declare to them, 'I never knew you; depart from me, you workers of lawlessness.'"

As Jesus said in His letter to the church in Sardis, "I will come like a thief, and you will not know at what hour I will come against you." There is nothing more important than making sure that we are alive in Christ. The church, just like the town of Sardis, had a glorious history but had become a shadow of what it once was.

They appeared alive; they were busy doing religious things. But Jesus knew their hearts, and the verdict was that there was no spiritual heartbeat. What about us? Do we just have the appearance of being alive, or is there spiritual vitality flowing through us? Jesus says, "Wake up!" I could come at any moment. Be ready, be faithful. Give yourself fully to Christ and the Kingdom. He who has an ear, let him hear what the Spirit says.

Closing Benediction: "May the church in America 'wake up.' May each of us examine our own hearts to discern if we are just busy with religious life or whether we truly are alive with the Spirit of God. Amen."

DAY 17

"Short But Scrappy"

Revelation 3:7-13

I was always one of the shortest kids in my class. There were times I would come home from school in tears because of kids making fun of my size. I always wished I had more height, but I had good speed, which helped make up for some of my vertical challenges in athletics.

According to my coaches, I also had plenty of heart. I was determined never to be outworked on the field or court. I had the following quote in my locker: "It's not the size of the dog in the fight, it's the size of the fight in the dog."[8]

When you're short, you have to be scrappy. I think that's a good description of the church we're looking at today. It was little in size but big in spirit. Sardis was a church that looked big on the outside but had little heart. The church in Philadelphia looked small on the outside but was big at heart. It was a scrappy church that stood its ground against the big, bad bullies of the world. Look at Revelation 3:7-13:

And to the angel of the church in Philadelphia write: 'The words of the holy one, the true one, who has the key of David, who opens and no one will shut, who shuts and no one opens.
"'I know your works. Behold, I have set before you an open

door, which no one is able to shut. I know that you have but little power, and yet you have kept my word and have not denied my name. Behold, I will make those of the synagogue of Satan who say that they are Jews and are not, but lie—behold, I will make them come and bow down before your feet, and they will learn that I have loved you. Because you have kept my word about patient endurance, I will keep you from the hour of trial that is coming on the whole world, to try those who dwell on the earth. I am coming soon. Hold fast what you have, so that no one may seize your crown. The one who conquers, I will make him a pillar in the temple of my God. Never shall he go out of it, and I will write on him the name of my God, and the name of the city of my God, the new Jerusalem, which comes down from my God out of heaven, and my own new name. He who has an ear, let him hear what the Spirit says to the churches.'

Maybe you feel puny amidst the ungodliness all around. Jesus said to "hold fast." You may have "little power," but in Christ's strength, you have resurrection power! He said to the church that "the synagogue of Satan" would come and bow down at their feet. It reminds me of the book of Esther where she goes from being an orphan to becoming queen. Haman tried to kill her people, the Jews, but instead, he ended up bowing at her feet, begging for his life.

Be encouraged today. We are on the winning team. We are on the side that will be exalted. As Jesus said in v. 12, we are "conquerors." Feeling small? Well, don't, for we are spiritually mighty. No power on earth can stand against us. We are the beloved sons and daughters of the King. Stand tall today.

Closing Benediction: "May we live out our true spiritual identity today. May we stand tall and strong against the Enemy. May we experience the power of the resurrection as we pursue the Kingdom of God. Amen."

DAY 18

"Spoiled Brats"

Revelation 3:14-22

I think all of us have experienced the awkwardness of being at the store as a three-year-old has a major meltdown. The annoying scream. The defiant backtalk. Throwing stuff on the ground. The parent counting to three, but everyone knows it won't work. It never does. You can try the two-and-a-half thing before three, but the kid won't fall for it.

Now, sometimes, it's just one of those days. As parents of six, we've had our moments in public, but that was a rarity, and normally, the threat of going to the bathroom for a "talk" fixed the situation. But there are times when you see a meltdown, and you know that three-year-old, thirty-pound preschooler is running the whole show at home. It should go without saying, but kids need correction in their lives.

Proverbs 13:24 says, "Whoever spares the rod hates his son, but he who loves him is diligent to discipline him." To not correct a child is actually hate, according to Proverbs. To discipline them is actually an act of love. A child needs to learn right and wrong. They need to learn there are consequences for wrong choices. It's helping prepare them for success in life and relationships.

In today's reading, we see a "bratty" little church that needed a good spanking from the Savior. Take a look at Revelation 3:14-22:

And to the angel of the church in Laodicea write: 'The words of the Amen, the faithful and true witness, the beginning of God's creation. "'I know your works: you are neither cold nor hot. Would that you were either cold or hot! So, because you are lukewarm, and neither hot nor cold, I will spit you out of my mouth. For you say, I am rich, I have prospered, and I need nothing, not realizing that you are wretched, pitiable, poor, blind, and naked. I counsel you to buy from me gold refined by fire, so that you may be rich, and white garments so that you may clothe yourself and the shame of your nakedness may not be seen, and salve to anoint your eyes, so that you may see. Those whom I love, I reprove and discipline, so be zealous and repent. Behold, I stand at the door and knock. If anyone hears my voice and opens the door, I will come in to him and eat with him, and he with me. The one who conquers, I will grant him to sit with me on my throne, as I also conquered and sat down with my Father on his throne. He who has an ear, let him hear what the Spirit says to the churches.'

This church was the "spoiled rich kids," who thought everything was fine because they were well off. But Jesus made it clear—they were anything but spiritually well off. They were poor and pitiful, because they had no passion for Christ. Jesus said they needed some pain to purify. They needed their eyes opened. Ultimately, they needed the discipline of the Lord.

Could it be true of us? Are we going through the motions, just "lukewarm?" God loves us enough to bring some correction into our lives to get our attention and get us in line with His will. Don't run from the discipline of the Lord. Embrace it. Hebrews 12:6 says: "For the Lord disciplines the one he loves, and chastises every son whom he receives." And besides, no one likes a spoiled little brat!

Closing Benediction: "May we pursue a passionate zeal for Christ. May we endure the discipline of the Lord to purify our faith. May we see the loving-kindness=k n-p2ju2 of the Lord behind it all. Amen."

DAY 19

"Puny Posers"

Revelation 3:1, 7, 14

I'm a fan of game shows. Some of my favorites are *Family Feud, Wheel of Fortune*, and *The Price is Right*. I dream of someday going on one of those shows and winning it all! It was before my time, but in the 60's, one of the most popular game shows was *To Tell the Truth*. The way the game worked was that after the host read the occupation of the main contestant, the celebrity panelists then would proceed to question the three contestants in an attempt to determine who the imposters were and who the contestant was that was telling the truth.

There are many so-called gods in the world, such as Buddha, Brahman, and Allah. And then there is God, existing in three persons—Father, Son, and Holy Spirit. So, how do we know who the real God and the "posers" are? Well, certainly, the Scriptures make it clear. Isaiah 44:6 says, "Thus says the Lord, the King of Israel and his Redeemer, the Lord of hosts: 'I am the first and I am the last; besides me there is no god.'"

Scripture teaches there are no other gods. Only God created the world and parted the seas. What other gods came in human form, miraculously, through a virgin, and died for mankind and defeated death? In today's passages, we see descriptions only the true God can possess. Look at the following verses in Revelation 3:

> V. 1: *"And to the angel of the church in Sardis write: 'The words of him who has the seven spirits of God and the seven stars."*

> V. 7: *"And to the angel of the church in Philadelphia write: 'The words of the holy one, the true one, who has the key of David, who opens and no one will shut, who shuts and no one opens.'"*

> V. 14: *"And to the angel of the church in Laodicea write: 'The words of the Amen, the faithful and true witness, the beginning of God's creation."*

How's that for a resume? He's over the churches. He's holy and true. He holds the key of David, and is the only one who opens and closes doors. He's the Amen. He's the faithful and true witness. He's the beginning of God's creation. Jesus is God, and all other claims pale in light of His glory and greatness.

How could we possibly bow to the gods of this world? The god of sex. The god of money. The god of power and prestige. The god of self.

In one of the funnier moments in *The Avengers*, The Incredible Hulk smashes Loki and says as he walks away, "Puny god." All other gods are posers. All other gods are puny. Let us bow a knee to the only true God, the creator of Heaven and Earth—the One we will worship for all eternity.

Closing Benediction: "May we refuse to bow a knee to anyone but God. May we live in the confidence that our Savior is greater than any gods of this world. And may it cause us to turn from sin and self, and follow Him with all of our hearts. Amen."

DAY 20

"Firm Foundation"

Revelation 3:5, 9-12, 20-21

The tallest building in the world is in Dubai and is called the Burj Khalifa. It's over 2,700 feet tall, which is over half a mile. To give you a little perspective, it's twice as tall as the Empire State Building. It's also home to the world's fastest elevator, which travels 40 MPH. The secret to the stability of this massive building is actually the part you don't see—it's the underground. Before construction began to raise the building, workers spent over a year digging and pouring the massive foundation that supports the building. The foundation weighs more than 110,000 tons.

The structure is safe because the foundation is solid. A structure is only as secure as its foundation. 1 Timothy 3:15 says the church is "the pillar and foundation of truth." The church is to be secure, no matter the changing winds of society, because it's built on the firm foundation of God's Word, whose cornerstone is Christ Jesus. In today's passages from Revelation 3, Jesus shares the rewards of those churches who stay true to His Word.

> V. 5: *"The one who conquers will be clothed thus in white garments, and I will never blot his name out of the book of life. I will confess his name before*

my Father and before his angels."

Vs. 9-12: *"Behold, I will make those of the synagogue of Satan who say that they are Jews and are not, but lie—behold, I will make them come and bow down before your feet, and they will learn that I have loved you. Because you have kept my word about patient endurance, I will keep you from the hour of trial that is coming on the whole world, to try those who dwell on the earth. I am coming soon. Hold fast what you have, so that no one may seize your crown. The one who conquers, I will make him a pillar in the temple of my God. Never shall he go out of it, and I will write on him the name of my God, and the name of the city of my God, the new Jerusalem, which comes down from my God out of heaven, and my own new name."*

Vs. 20-21: *"Behold, I stand at the door and knock. If anyone hears my voice and opens the door, I will come in to him and eat with him, and he with me. The one who conquers, I will grant him to sit with me on my throne, as I also conquered and sat down with my Father on his throne."*

All kinds of great rewards are mentioned in these verses, but I just want to mention one of them from verse 12: "The one who conquers, I will make him a pillar in the temple of my God." A pillar is known for having a firm foundation. This metaphor would have resonated in the church of Philadelphia. Why? Because in 17 A.D., a mighty earthquake destroyed the city.

It would have been a great comfort to be reminded that their heavenly dwelling was a pillar, a home that could never be destroyed. And it's true for us. On our worst days, remember that we have a bright future with an eternal home, and nothing can ever destroy that.

Closing Benediction: "May the hope of Heaven encourage us today. May the changing winds of society not sway us to the right or the left. May we stay rooted, strong in our faith and the truth of God's Word. Amen."

DAY 21

"The Throne"

Revelation 4:1-2

The story is about a king sitting on his throne, meeting with his council of noblemen, advisers, and ministers of state. When, all of a sudden, there was a loud banging at the door. All eyes turned as the door swung wide open, and a boy ran into the room.

One of the king's guardsmen tried to stop the boy from running in. "Hold on there, little one!" he shouted. "You're disturbing the council of the king." The boy smiled and said, "He's your king. But he's my daddy!" And the boy jumped into the wide open arms of his father, the king.

May we never lose the wonder of being the beloved children of the King who have access to His throne room. Only when we enter Heaven will we truly understand just how magnificent and glorious it is to enter the King's presence. The Apostle John had the incredible privilege of receiving a vision of God, sitting on His throne in Heaven. Look at Revelation 4:1-2:

> *After this I looked, and behold, a door standing open in heaven! And the first voice, which I had heard speaking to me like a trumpet, said, "Come up here, and I will show you what must take place after this." At once I was in the*

*Spirit, and behold, a throne stood in heaven, with
one seated on the throne.*

The "after this" in verse one refers to the vision given of Jesus' messages for seven specific churches in Asia Minor, which we looked at in chapters two and three. In the book's opening chapter in v. 19, Jesus said to John: "Write therefore the things that you have seen, those that are and those that are to take place after this."

John has received a vision of Jesus in chapter 1. That's the "things that you have seen." Jesus gave the seven churches the message in chapters two and three. That's the "those that are." And now, Jesus will provide a vision of future events in chapters four through twenty-two. That's the "those that are to take place." In preparation for the vision of future things, John receives a vision of God (chapter four), as God the Holy Creator, and then a vision of Jesus (chapter five), as Jesus the Redeemer who is Worthy.

Before John is to receive the vision of the people and places that are part of the future, he receives the vision, perhaps as a reminder, that what matters most about the future is the Personhood of God. Heaven will be the throne room of God where we will walk and worship perfectly with a holy God, worthy of all our worship.

I believe our generation needs a fresh vision of who God is, a reminder of how incredibly holy and glorious He is. Otherwise, we will continue down the road of worshiping lesser things. May this week of looking at the throne of God recapture the wonder and awe of being chosen as children who have access to the Father's throne.

Closing Benediction: "May we come to God as children in love with their Father. May we slow down our lives enough to enter His presence each day. May God give us a renewed vision of who He is. Amen."

DAY 22

"Brilliant And Beautiful"

Revelation 4:3-4

I have had the privilege of traveling to many places around the world. Sometimes for pleasure and sometimes for ministry. I've stood on top of the Rocky Mountains and the Pocono Mountains and the Appalachian Mountains. I've viewed the sunset over the waters of beaches in Florida, California, and South and North Carolina.

I've hiked through the Amazon jungles of Ecuador. I've driven through vineyards and stood atop Table Mountain in Cape Town, South Africa. I've ridden a speedboat on the Mediterranean Sea. I've sat on a rooftop in Sicily, watching the bright glow of lava spew out of Mount Etna.

All to say, I've seen some of the most beautiful parts of creation throughout the world, yet all of it will dim in comparison to standing in the brilliant, beautiful presence of the God of all creation. The Apostle John had this incredible opportunity while imprisoned on the Island of Patmos. Look at Revelation 4:3-4:

> *And he who sat there had the appearance of jasper and carnelian, and around the throne was a rainbow that had the appearance of an emerald. Around the throne were*

twenty-four thrones, and seated on the thrones were twenty-four elders, clothed in white garments, with golden crowns on their heads.

The jasper is a clear stone, like a diamond, and the carnelian, also known as a ruby, is a red-colored stone. The jasper and the carnelian were the first and the last of the 12 gemstones worn on the high priest's breast (Exodus 28:17-21). Exodus 28:21 says the following about the twelve stones: "There shall be twelve stones with their names according to the names of the sons of Israel." The throne having the appearance of jasper and carnelian may mean to depict that God is the God of Israel.

These stones will be the foundation of the future New Jerusalem (Revelation 21:19-20). God is not only the God of Israel; he is the God of the New Jerusalem. His brilliance will light up the holy city of God. The beauty of this city will be unlike any other.

His throne was encircled by a rainbow, marked with green, like emeralds. God's presence was filled with the colors of creation, and it included a rainbow–God's covenant promise not to destroy the world with a flood. This vision of God reminds us that God keeps His promises to His people.

Twenty-four elders sat on twenty-four smaller thrones as they worshiped the God of the one true throne. The twenty-four elders wore the crowns of victors like at the Greek games. It depicted that these elders had been judged and rewarded. God is a God who rewards. Who were these twenty-four elders?

Good question.

Some see them as the twelve patriarchs of the Old Testament and the twelve apostles of the New Testament. Some see them as a superior order of angels. Whoever they were, this beautiful vision of God's brilliance will lead to magnificent creatures bowing and worshiping an even more magnificent Creator. This is a picture of our future. A day when we will stand in the presence of a brilliant and beautiful God as we exist in the most beautiful place the mind could ever imagine.

Closing Benediction: "May we live with our eyes focused on our brilliant and beautiful eternal home. May we take time to celebrate God's glorious creation, a glimpse of what glory will look like. Amen."

DAY 23

"A Beautiful Trembling"

Revelation 4:5-6a

God's creation can evoke feelings of calm and rest, such as when we look at a sunset or blue calm waters. But it can also evoke fear and trembling. For some, fear and trembling come at the sound of thunder or the sirens warning of a tornado. I live in an area where tornadoes have touched down over the years.

In fact, the fourth worst tornado in U.S. history occurred where I live (Elkhart, Indiana) on Palm Sunday in 1965. Over 130 people were killed and 1,300 injured. One of my best friends growing up had a dad who was paralyzed from the storm. I remember my dad telling me stories about cars and animals blown into trees.

I've never actually been in a tornado, and I hope I never will be. But I am sure, if I ever was, fear and trembling would be my response. Now imagine for a second a storm in Heaven. How would that make us feel? Well, John the Apostle could answer that question. He experienced it. Take a look at Revelation 4:5-6a:

From the throne came flashes of lightning, and rumblings and peals of thunder, and before the throne were burning seven torches of fire, which are the seven spirits of God, and before the throne there was as it were a sea of glass, like crystal.

In these verses, John continues to give a description of this vision of God on His throne in heaven. It is not a depiction of God Himself, for He is Spirit, not of flesh and bone. But it is a depiction of what surrounds the throne of God. And it is both beautiful and frightening. It includes beautiful brightness and a rainbow, but also lightning and thunder and fire.

If verses three and four remind us of His beauty, verses five and six remind us of His awesome power. If the previous verses remind us to worship, these verses remind us to be in reverential awe. God is beautiful and powerful. He is the God of the still waters, and He is the God of the crashing waves.

When we come into the presence of God in prayer and praise, we need to remember to adore His beauty and show reverence for His power. May we take comfort that He makes beauty out of ashes, and may we take courage that His power has disarmed the power of the enemy.

Closing Benediction: "May we live with the balance of seeing God's beauty, and being in awe of His power and majesty. May we come humbly into His presence and live boldly as a result of it. Amen."

DAY 24

"Mind The Gap"

Revelation 4:6b-8

If you lived in London, you would be very familiar with the term "mind the gap." Whenever you get on or off the rail trains in London, you hear the recorded voice reminding everyone of the dangerous gap that awaits distracted travelers. The phrase has become so popular, it's been the title of songs, used in video games, and can be found on tourist t-shirts.

Mind the gap. That's a good phrase to remember and repeat as we journey in the world on this side of Heaven. There is a significant gap between our sinfulness and God's total and complete holiness. Since the Garden of Eden, when sin entered the world, a gap has existed between us and God. Sinfulness and holiness don't mix. John is reminded of this in Revelation 4:6b-8:

And around the throne, on each side of the throne, are four living creatures, full of eyes in front and behind: the first living creature like a lion, the second living creature like an ox, the third living creature with the face of a man, and the fourth living creature like an eagle in flight. And the four living creatures, each of them with six wings, are full of eyes all around and within, and day and night they never cease to say, "Holy, holy, holy, is the Lord God

Almighty, who was and is and is to come!"

While there are a lot of interpretations of what these creatures represent, the simplest explanation is that these are angelic beings whose eyes have seen the holiness of God and can't help but sing about it. It is very similar to the scene in Isaiah 6 when the angels also sang of the holiness of God.

We need a renewed vision of what holiness is and why it matters so much. Recapturing God's holiness and our need for holiness will help us loosen our grip on sin and deepen our urge for glory. And as we will see in Revelation 5, all of this is possible because of the death and resurrection of Jesus. His blood bridges the gap between our sinfulness and God's holiness.

Charles Spurgeon sums it up well: "I believe that great holiness sets us free from the love of this world and makes us ready to depart. By great holiness, I mean great horror of sin and great longing after perfect purity."[9]

Closing Benediction: "May we hate sin like God hates sin. May we yearn for the holiness of God in our lives. May we daily give thanks that the blood of Jesus makes a life with God possible. Amen."

DAY 25

"Unfading Glory"

Revelation 4:9-11

We've all heard the phrase, "The glory days." And when we've used the phrase, it's normally in the context of having been removed from them many years ago. In the glory days, I ran fast and free. I had boundless energy. I could play or work all day with no fear of pain when I woke up the next morning. In the glory days, I didn't need to check to see if my hair had rescinded. I didn't need to watch what I ate. I didn't need to write things down for fear of forgetting them. The glory days.

We've seen the boxer who fights one too many fights. The ballplayer who plays one too many seasons, living under the delusion that their skills had not diminished. You don't have to be a top athlete to see the effects of fading glory. Since the Fall in the Garden of Eden, everything on earth deteriorates. Everything on earth is under the curse of sin. Death and deterioration are the norm. If our hope rests only in this world, what a pity our lives would be. Praise be to God that it doesn't.

With God, every day is a glory day. There is no fading glory with God. He is the same yesterday, today, and forever. Heaven is not under the curse of sin. In fact, there is no sin in Heaven. Worthy is God to be praised for His unfading glory. John had an awesome privilege to see a vision depicting God in glory.

Look at Revelation 4:9-11:

And whenever the living creatures give glory and honor and thanks to him who is seated on the throne, who lives forever and ever, the twenty-four elders fall down before him who is seated on the throne and worship him who lives forever and ever. They cast their crowns before the throne, saying, "Worthy are you, our Lord and God, to receive glory and honor and power, for you created all things, and by your will they existed and were created."

Whoever these twenty-four elders were, their response to the unfading glory of God was to cast their crowns before Him and worship His name. Crowns represent achievement. It is a symbol of victory. When these beings stood before God's throne, all they could think to do was give God their crowns.

It's so easy to be consumed on earth by pursuing personal achievements, to gain crowns for ourselves, yet these crowns fade away. We need to be captured by the glory of God in Heaven. It will redirect our actions and motives and priorities toward eternal things.

Jesus put it this way in Matthew 6:19-20: "Do not lay up for yourselves treasures on earth, where moth and rust destroy and where thieves break in and steal, but lay up for yourselves treasures in Heaven, where neither moth nor rust destroys and where thieves do not break in and steal." Let us serve for unfading crowns that we will lay down before the unfading glory of God.

Closing Benediction: "May we live for the unfading glory of God. May we not give ourselves to the crowns of earth that moth and rust destroy, that thieves break in and steal. Amen."

DAY 26

"Tears In Heaven"
Revelation 5:1-4

Eric Clapton, one of the most influential guitarists of all time, wrote a #1 hit song in 1991 called "Tears in Heaven." It was written shortly after the tragic death of his four-year-old son, who fell from a window of the 53rd floor of a New York apartment. He wrote the song as a means of coping with his grief.

When we think about Heaven, we don't think of tears. And yet, in the vision John receives in Revelation 5, we see "tears in Heaven." It's the only time there will ever be tears in glory. Look at verses 1-4:

Then I saw in the right hand of him who was seated on the throne a scroll written within and on the back, sealed with seven seals. And I saw a mighty angel proclaiming with a loud voice, "Who is worthy to open the scroll and break its seals?" And no one in heaven or on earth or under the earth was able to open the scroll or to look into it, and I began to weep loudly because no one was found worthy to open the scroll or to look into it.

What was it that caused John to shed tears in this vision? It seemed no one would be worthy to open the scroll. When we get to the next verse, we will see there is indeed one able to open the scroll, but at the moment, John was unaware of that.

We've all shed tears. Some cry easily, and some rarely cry, but we all do, because God created us with tears. And there is value in them. Psalm 56:8 says, "You have kept count of my tossings; put my tears in your bottle. Are they not in your book?"

I think what the Psalmist means is our tears are not wasted. God will redeem our tears and the pain behind them. I think the scroll was the deed to the Kingdom of Heaven. It will open the inheritance promised to the children of God. If the deed isn't opened, redemption will not happen.

Maybe it feels that way sometimes in your life, that there's no future glory, just day after day of groaning. Well, as we will see in the next verse, we have a Savior who will open up the sealed scroll. And forevermore, we will be joint heirs with Jesus for eternity.

The end of Revelation reminds us that the day will come indeed when there will be no tears. Revelation 21:4: "He will wipe away every tear from their eyes, and death shall be no more, neither shall there be mourning, nor crying, nor pain anymore, for the former things have passed away."

Closing Benediction: "May we remember the next time we shed tears that God never lets them go to waste. May we remember that Heaven will redeem the pain behind our tears because of what Jesus has done for us. Amen."

DAY 27

"To The Victor Go The Spoils"

Revelation 5:5-7

To the victor go the spoils. This term was first used by New York Senator William Marcy, referring to the victory of Andrew Jackson in the presidential election of 1828. The phrase means that the "spoils" are the goods or benefits taken from the loser in a competition, election, or military victory.

From Julius Caesar to Genghis Khan, the spoils they would receive motivated leaders to conquer other lands. While there may have been noble reasons for battle, in many cases, it just came down to the desire to take from the enemy.

Satan has always desired what God has—glory and power. When Jesus came to the earth, Satan tried to thwart His plan for redeeming mankind. He probably thought he won when Jesus was crucified. But Jesus conquered the cross. And that victory had eternal consequences. Look at Revelation 5:5-7:

"And one of the elders said to me, "Weep no more; behold, the Lion of the tribe of Judah, the Root of David, has conquered, so that he can open the scroll and its seven seals." And between the throne and the four living creatures and among the elders I saw a Lamb standing, as though it had been slain, with seven horns and with seven eyes, which are

the seven spirits of God sent out into all the earth. And he went and took the scroll from the right hand of him who was seated on the throne."

Jesus' death covered our sins, but it was His resurrection that gave us new life. So many Christians are clueless about the depth of spiritual power available to them because Jesus defeated Satan. To the victor go the spoils. We now fight from victory, not for victory.

Jewish kings came from the line of Judah, so Jesus, who came from the line of Judah, the "Root of David," is king on earth, and as we see in today's verses, He is the king in Heaven. So the question is: Are we submitting to the King of Kings daily? Are we seeing sin conquered in our lives?

To the victor go the spoils. We may lose some skirmishes along the way, but the war has been won, and someday, we will experience all of the riches of Heaven.

Closing Benediction: "May the reality that we are conquerors in Christ give us confidence in our daily fight against Satan and sin. May we submit to our King this week, for only He is worthy of all that we have. Amen."

DAY 28

"Not Wasted"

Revelation 5:8-10

There are things you want to be first in and things you don't want to be first in. The United States is first in something we would rather not be first in. We are the world's most wasteful country, and the runner-up isn't even close. The United States accounts for only about four percent of the world's population yet generates twelve percent of the world's solid waste. The average American produces more than 1,700 pounds of waste a year.[10]

My point is that we throw out a lot of stuff. We waste. But I have some great news if you are a follower of Jesus. There are things in our lives that are never wasted. As mentioned before, tears are not wasted. God bottles up our tears. They will never be thrown out.

A second very important thing that is not wasted is our prayers. Revelation 5:8-10 talks about the Savior and how we can be part of the eternal kingdom of Heaven, and our prayers have some type of role in it. Let's look at the verses:

And when he had taken the scroll, the four living creatures and the twenty-four elders fell down before the Lamb, each holding a harp, and golden bowls full of incense, which are the prayers of the saints. And they sang a new song, saying, 'Worthy are you to take the scroll and to open its seals, for you were slain, and by your blood you ransomed people for God from every tribe and language and people and nation, and you have made them a kingdom and priests to our God, and they shall reign on the earth.'"

What a thought, that our prayers are kept in "golden bowls full of incense." God stores up both our tears and our prayers. What a good and gracious God we have. Consider these words by William Newell: "Some day it will be found that every soul that has been saved, every blessing any saint has received, every thwarting of Satan, every victory for God, as well as the consummation of our Lord's taking over the kingdom — all have been brought about through the saints' prayers, inspired of God as essential elements in His great, all comprehensive plan."[11]

Wow! I don't know what will if that doesn't motivate us to pray. God is sovereign, and it's the work of Jesus that saves, but somehow, our prayers play a part in it all.

Closing Benediction: "May we treat prayer with the utmost importance. May we never forget that God is in the redemption business. May we stay humble, knowing it's the shed blood of Christ that pays for our sins. Amen."

DAY 29

"Jesus > Angels"

Revelation 5:11-12

There's a story about angels that takes place during World War II. The plane of two pilots was heavily damaged by gunfire and began falling to earth, when all of a sudden, one of the pilots looked out of the window and saw a huge angel on one wing of the plane. He then looked out the opposite window and saw another angel on the other wing. According to the pilots, the angels helped land the plane, and their lives were spared.

True story? I have no idea, but it certainly could have happened. One of the roles of an angel is to help believers. Hebrews 1:14 says, "Are they not all ministering spirits sent out to serve for the sake of those who are to inherit salvation?" The word 'angel' means 'messenger,' so another role of angels is to deliver messages from God.

We know, according to Ephesians 6, that angels also fight in spiritual warfare against Satan and the fallen angels. And, of course, angels worship God. But not just God the Father, they also worship Jesus. Hebrews talks about Jesus being greater than angels. Hebrews 1:4 says the following about Jesus, "having become as much superior to angels as the name he has inherited is more excellent than theirs."

Today's passage is a reminder that these magnificent spiritual creatures will worship the greatness of our Savior. Look at Revelation 5:11-12:

"Then I looked, and I heard around the throne and the living creatures and the elders the voice of many angels, numbering myriads of myriads and thousands of thousands, saying with a loud voice, 'Worthy is the Lamb who was slain, to receive power and wealth and wisdom and might and honor and glory and blessing!'"

Humans are not worthy to open the scroll. Nor are the twenty-four elders. Not even the mighty angels. Only Jesus was worthy to open the scroll. Can you imagine the scene in Heaven? Myriads means "countless." Countless angels worshipping Jesus.

Hebrews 12:22 puts it this way: "But you have come to Mount Zion and to the city of the living God, the heavenly Jerusalem, and to innumerable angels in festal gathering." How glorious Heaven will be. An eternal festival of joy, praising the Lamb that is worthy to receive power and wealth and wisdom and might and honor and glory and blessing!

Closing Benediction: "May we be encouraged that angels are all around us. And may we be filled with great hope, knowing that we will join them in worshiping our Savior forever. Amen."

DAY 30

"Cape Of Good Hope"

Revelation 5:13-14

On a mission trip to South Africa years ago, we stopped and visited the Cape of Good Hope near Cape Town. At the time, I wasn't aware of the history of the place. I later discovered that one of the early explorers, Bartolomeu Dias, went around the cape on a stormy sea. His ship threatened to go to pieces, so he called it the Cape of Storms. But Vasco da Gama, who came later, changed the name to the Cape of Good Hope, because he saw ahead of him the jewels and treasures of India.

This side of Heaven will have its share of storms. None of us are immune to them. It's part of the curse that sin brought. And if this life is all there is, what a sad reality that would be. But it isn't. We have a heavenly home waiting for us. And it's the ultimate "Cape of Good Hope."

The Apostle John experienced the "Cape of Storms." He was probably in his nineties and was imprisoned for his commitment to the gospel. The vision of Heaven in Revelation 5 must have been a great reminder of the eternal hope of Heaven. Let's look at how the chapter ends in verses 13-14:

> *And I heard every creature in heaven and on earth and under the earth and in the sea, and all that is in them,*

> *saying, "To him who sits on the throne and to the Lamb be blessing and honor and glory and might forever and ever!" And the four living creatures said, "Amen!" and the elders fell down and worshiped."*

Forever and ever, we will live to worship Jesus. Forever and ever, we will experience joyful bliss. We will never sin. We will never hurt. We will never get sick, and we will never die. As the song goes, "When we all get to heaven, what a day of rejoicing that will be! When we all see Jesus, we'll sing and shout the victory!"[12] Next time you're going through the storm, remember that this, too, shall pass.

Don't ignore the storm, but also make sure to look beyond it. Remember the good hope of Heaven. That's our final destination. A place of perfection. In this world, we will have troubles, but in glory, we will live in perfect peace!

Closing Benediction: "May we sing and shout the victory today in our lives. May we face the storms of life with courage, knowing that 'this too will pass.' Amen."

DAY 31

"The Four Horsemen"
Revelation 6:1-4

I live close to Notre Dame University. The Fighting Irish have a rich football history, from the phrase "Win one for the Gipper" to the "Play like a champion" pre-game ritual to the inspiring story of Rudy. Part of Notre Dame's lore includes "The Four Horsemen of Notre Dame."

It was the name given to four players who played in the backfield of coach Knute Rockne's 1924 team. The nickname was coined by legendary sports writer Grantland Rice after Notre Dame's upset victory over a strong Army team. Rice penned these famous words that day in the New York Herald Tribune:

Outlined against a blue-gray October sky, the Four Horsemen rode again. In dramatic lore their names are Famine, Pestilence, Destruction, and Death. These are only aliases. Their real names are Stuhldreher, Miller, Crowley and Layden.[13]

Grantland Rice was clearly using the description in Revelation 6, which refers to the Tribulation. The Tribulation is a seven-year period in which God will judge the world for sin. In this chapter, we see the first of three sets of judgments. This set of judgments is the Seal Judgments. And in the first eight verses, we see four of them, the "Four Horsemen of the Apocalypse." Today, we'll take a look at the first two. Look at Revelation 6:1-4:

Now I watched when the Lamb opened one of the seven seals, and I heard one of the four living creatures say with a voice like thunder, "Come!" And I looked, and behold, a white horse! And its rider had a bow, and a crown was given to him, and he came out conquering, and to conquer. When he opened the second seal, I heard the second living creature say, "Come!" And out came another horse, bright red. Its rider was permitted to take peace from the earth, so that people should slay one another, and he was given a great sword."

There are all kinds of interpretations of Revelation and of the End Times. I believe Jesus will rapture Christians before the Tribulation, and the Tribulation will be "hell on earth." I believe the first seal judgment describes the Antichrist, a figure influenced by Satan who will be received as the world leader of a one world order. Notice there are no arrows for the bow. He will come proclaiming peace. But, based on Daniel 9, he will eventually show his true colors and desecrate the Temple, which will be rebuilt in Jerusalem.

Peace on the earth will be short-lived. There will be war after war. The red horse, I believe, represents bloodshed—the result of wars breaking out throughout the world. Things will get progressively worse, as we will see in the rest of the Seal Judgments and the other two sets of judgments, the Trumpet and Bowl Judgments. We are going on a journey in the upcoming chapters that may make some feel uncomfortable. But understand, God is a righteous God, and evil will not go unpunished. The world is accountable to God, and only those who bow a knee to Jesus will escape the righteous punishment of God.

Closing Benediction: "May we grasp the seriousness of sin. May we be incredibly grateful that God's grace saves us from the coming wrath because of the finished work of Christ. Amen."

DAY 32

"Rags To Riches"

Revelation 6:5-8

There have been a number of inspirational sports movies over the years. One of my favorites is *Cinderella Man*. It's the true story of heavyweight boxer Jim Braddock. The boxer earned his nickname from his fairytale-like rise from a poor local fighter to heavyweight champion of the world.

Braddock had fought for the title in 1929 but lost a heartbreaking fifteen-round decision. That same year, the stock market crashed, and he went from title contender to one of millions of poor Americans trying to survive The Great Depression. Desperate to put food on the table, he grudgingly accepted government handouts and stood in breadlines. At one point, it got so bad, he asked for money from friends.

However, his fortunes began to change in 1934. Intended to simply be a stepping stone in "Corn" Griffin's boxing career, and with twenty-five losses on his record, Braddock upset the heavy favorite, knocking him out in the third round. He followed that up with another upset by defeating future light heavyweight champion John Henry Lewis.

As a result, Jim Braddock was given a title fight with the mighty champion Max Baer. Considered nothing more than a journeyman fighter, Braddock was picked by Baer's team as an easy payday for the champion. But on June 13, 1935, at Madison Square Garden Bowl, the 10-to-1 underdog scored one of the greatest upsets in boxing history—a true rags-to-riches story.

The backdrop of this story was The Great Depression, a dark and dreary time in our nation's history. Braddock survived the poverty and went on to experience earthly glory. The seven-year Tribulation will be a time of even greater darkness and dreariness. But for those who find Christ during this time, it will eventually lead to heavenly glory. Let's look at Revelation 6:5-8:

When he opened the third seal, I heard the third living creature say, "Come!" And I looked, and behold, a black horse! And its rider had a pair of scales in his hand. And I heard what seemed to be a voice in the midst of the four living creatures, saying, "A quart of wheat for a denarius, and three quarts of barley for a denarius, and do not harm the oil and wine!" When he opened the fourth seal, I heard the voice of the fourth living creature say, "Come!" And I looked, and behold, a pale horse! And its rider's name was Death, and Hades followed him. And they were given authority over a fourth of the earth, to kill with sword and with famine and with pestilence and by wild beasts of the earth.

Today, we're looking at the third and fourth seal judgment, also known as the third and fourth "Horsemen of the Apocalypse." In the opening years of the Tribulation, there will be famine and poverty, represented by the black horse, which will lead to economic inflation. The combination of this and war will lead to one-fourth of the world's population killed, which is represented by the pale horse. We're talking about the potential of over a billion people dying within the first couple of years of the Tribulation.

While this may evoke sadness, the truth is, God limits His wrath for sin on earth to seven years. As we will see later in the book, all the redeemed, including those who find Christ during the Tribulation, will be ushered into God's glorious kingdom, known as the Millennium, which will include Christ reigning on earth for a thousand years. And after that, for all eternity.

This chapter harshly reminds us of the reality of sin's consequences. May it also remind us that God, in His infinite mercy and grace, will end the punishment and restore redeemed people to His kingdom. It will be the ultimate rags-to-riches story.

Closing Benediction: "May we be thankful we have food to eat and that death only leads to real life. May we stay humble before God, knowing that He has chosen to spare us from the price of sin and instead allow us to be His beloved children. Amen."

DAY 33

"Slain For The Word"

Revelation 6:9-11

In a sermon by J.C. Ryle, the true story was told of Hugh Latimer, a Protestant reformer in England in the sixteenth century. He was a gifted teacher and was once asked to speak before King Henry VIII of England. In preparing his sermon, he sensed God was calling him to deliver a message that would not make the king happy. He was determined to obey God no matter the cost.

He began his sermon by saying, "Latimer! Latimer! Do you remember that you are speaking before the high and mighty King Henry VIII; who has power to command you to be sent to prison, and who can have your head cut off, if it pleases him? Will you not take care to say nothing that will offend royal ears?"

Latimer paused and continued, "Latimer! Latimer! Do you not remember that you are speaking before the King of kings and Lord of lords; before Him, at whose throne Henry VIII will stand; before Him, to whom one day you will have to give account yourself? Latimer! Latimer! Be faithful to your Master, and declare all of God's Word."[14]

As followers of Christ, we must choose whether to follow

Christ or the world, even at the expense of our own lives. Latimer faced that choice, and his answer was clear: He would obey and follow Christ. He stood for truth and boldly preached God's Word. Eventually, Henry's daughter, Queen Mary, martyred him.

We have a rich history of men and women who have been martyred for their uncompromising commitment to Christ. In fact, there have been an estimated seventy million Christians martyred since the time of Christ. During the Tribulation, there will be an unparalleled amount of individuals who will come to know Christ and be killed for it. Revelation 6:9-11 talks about this. Let's take a look:

When he opened the fifth seal, I saw under the altar the souls of those who had been slain for the word of God and for the witness they had borne. They cried out with a loud voice, "O Sovereign Lord, holy and true, how long before you will judge and avenge our blood on those who dwell on the earth?" Then they were each given a white robe and told to rest a little longer, until the number of their fellow servants and their brothers should be complete, who were to be killed as they themselves had been.

The fifth Seal Judgment was the slaying of believers who refused to deny the faith. God will avenge their blood and bring them home to glory. While this passage refers to the time of the Tribulation, I believe it's still a source of encouragement for us today. We have a God who rights the wrongs, who punishes the wicked. We have nothing to fear. May the words of Jesus from

Matthew 10:26-28 be an encouragement:

> *So have no fear of them, for nothing is covered that will not be revealed, or hidden that will not be known. What I tell you in the dark, say in the light, and what you hear whispered, proclaim on the housetops. And do not fear those who kill the body but cannot kill the soul. Rather fear him who can destroy both soul and body in hell.*

Closing Benediction: "May we be thankful for the rich heritage we have of men and women who have been willing to give up their lives for the cause of Christ. May we have the courage to risk all to stand for Christ in a culture that desperately needs Him. Amen."

DAY 34
"The Earth Will Quake"
Revelation 6:12-14

One of the deadliest earthquakes the world has ever known occurred on January 23rd, 1556, in Shaanxi, China. The earthquake only lasted a few seconds; however, it leveled mountains, altered the path of rivers, ignited fires, and caused massive flooding.

The earthquake affected a hundred different countries, many of them reporting the deaths of over half their populations. In total, this one earthquake only lasted a few seconds but left over 800,000 people dead. Even as destructive as this earthquake was, it pales compared to an earthquake that will come upon the land during the Tribulation. Let's read about it in Revelation 6:12-14:

> *When he opened the sixth seal, I looked, and behold, there was a great earthquake, and the sun became black as sackcloth, the full moon became like blood, and the stars of the sky fell to the earth as the fig tree sheds its winter fruit when shaken by a gale. The sky vanished like a scroll that is being rolled up, and every mountain and island was removed from its place.*

This earthquake will disrupt the entire planet. It's actually one of three that will occur during the Tribulation. This first one will impact the sun, moon, and stars in the sky. John is using symbolic language here to describe a terrifying cosmological disaster. It could be, when John says, "the sun became black as sackcloth," that volcanic eruptions will spew ash and gasses into the atmosphere that will cause the sun to appear black. When it says, "the full moon became like blood and the stars of the sky fell to earth," Charles Swindoll writes that this could mean that "putrid air distorts the color of the moon, and the heavens rain down meteors."[15]

And people can't run and hide in the mountains or on an island, because they're gone! Nature's fury will be unleashed beyond anything the world has seen. In the Garden of Eden, God created the most beautiful world. When Adam and Eve sinned, a curse came upon mankind and upon creation itself. While creation still had beauty, it was also tainted by the curse, which caused catastrophes and death over the years. Nature will cause intense pain and heartache during the Tribulation.

However, the day will come when the believer will no longer experience pain and heartache, and nature will never cause pain or heartache. When we reach the end of the Book of Revelation and God establishes the "New Heavens and Earth," we will walk in the glorious presence of God and His Son Jesus, and we will experience creation like it once was in the Garden—pure and beautiful, without blemish.

In 1706, English minister and hymn writer Isaac Watts wrote, *There is a Land of Pure Delight*. I'll close with the first verse:

"There is a land of pure delight, where saints immortal reign; infinite day excludes the night, and pleasures banish pain."[16] Oh, saints, what a day it will be when the land will bring pure delight, and pleasures banish pain.

Closing Benediction: "May we take time to soak in God's beautiful creation this week. When we see the effects of the curse on creation, may we be reminded that someday, all the consequences of sin will be removed from the earth. Amen."

DAY 35

"A Frightening Being To Behold"
Revelation 6:15-17

One of my favorite shows as a kid was *The Incredible Hulk*. The show was based on the Stan Lee comic character he created in 1962. The character has dissociative identity disorder (DID), which is represented by the alter Hulk as a green-skinned, muscular humanoid who possesses a limitless degree of physical strength, and the alter Dr. Bruce Banner, a gentle, withdrawn physicist.

No one would look at Bruce Banner and tremble with fear. He was a physically weak, nerdy character. But when he transformed into the Hulk, he was a frightening being to behold. Similarly, when Jesus walked the earth, according to Isaiah 53:2, "he had no form or majesty that we should look at him, and no beauty that we should desire him."

Jesus was not physically impressive. He entered the city the last week of His life on earth, meek and mild. On the surface, it looked like He left Earth with a whimper, not a bang. The resurrection changed all that. And just wait until we get to Revelation 19!

Revelation 6 is also a reminder that Jesus may be meek and mild, but He's also mighty, and if you don't know Christ, He will be terrifying. Part of the reason for the Tribulation is for the rebellious to experience the wrath of Jesus. Look at Revelation 6:15-17:

> *Then the kings of the earth and the great ones and the generals and the rich and the powerful, and everyone, slave and free, hid themselves in the caves and among the rocks of the mountains, calling to the mountains and rocks, "Fall on us and hide us from the face of him who is seated on the throne, and from the wrath of the Lamb, for the great day of their wrath has come, and who can stand?"*

These verses may be uncomfortable to read. It's not the image of Jesus we typically think about, "the wrath of the Lamb," the One who sends the mightiest, most powerful kings and generals running to the caves in fear. I think it's important to remember it's not the believers but the unbelievers. The wrath of the Lamb is for those who have refused to bow a knee to Christ.

These verses can actually be a source of comfort. The world is not filled with just rainbows, lollipops, and pixie dust. Life is filled with wickedness and corruption. Just watch the nightly news—school shootings, corrupt politicians, wars, and genocide. It's easy to lose hope. It's easy to feel defeated, but nothing could be further from the truth. All the ugly we see in the world will end, and all who are behind it will pay the price. The wrath of the Lamb will subside, and paradise will be our forever home, with Jesus as our forever leader.

Closing Benediction: "May we never fear the attack of the Evil

One nor the attacks of the people of the world because we have the Lamb of God to whom all will bow before. May we live as conquerors in light of having a Savior who conquered us through His grace. Amen."

DAY 36

"Sealed"

Revelation 7:1-3

My mother-in-law likes to make jam, which is great because my family gets to reap the benefits of her hobby. There is nothing like homemade jam. It's a pretty simple process of preserving it. You pour wax over the top of the preserves until it's at the brim of the jar. Then, you place a rubber-lined lid on tight. The wax and the vacuum caused by the cooling preserves seal that jar so tight that it could sit for years, and the jam would still be good. Why? The jam is sealed; it's protected and preserved.

Did you know when we give our lives to Christ as Lord and Savior, we are sealed for eternity? Ephesians 1:13-14 says, "In him you also, when you heard the word of truth, the gospel of your salvation, and believed in him, were sealed with the promised Holy Spirit, who is the guarantee of our inheritance until we acquire possession of it, to the praise of his glory."

The Holy Spirit seals us until we get to glory. Isn't that amazing? We are protected by God and preserved until the Lord's return. In our passage for today, we see another group of individuals who are sealed during the time known as the Tribulation. Look at Revelation 7:1-3:

After this I saw four angels standing at the four corners of the earth, holding back the four winds of the earth, that no wind might blow on earth or sea or against any tree. Then I saw another angel ascending from the rising of the sun, with the seal of the living God, and he called with a loud voice to the four angels who had been given power to harm earth and sea, saying "Do not harm the earth or the sea or the trees, until we have sealed the servants of our God on their foreheads."

God will give these angels the authority to restrain and implement His judgment. One of the angels instructs to wait with the judgments until these select individuals have a seal of protection put on their foreheads, whether it be literally or figuratively. They are protected from death during the Tribulation. In the next verse, we will see who, specifically, these sealed individuals are. But for today, simply know that they are individuals who come to a saving knowledge of Jesus during the early stages of the Tribulation. And, as we will see, they have a special task God has for them that significantly impacts the kingdom of God.

We live in a time before the Tribulation, but God has also sealed us, not from physical death, but a protection of our salvation. God has also given us a task until we experience the glories of Heaven. We are to embody the gospel in our lives and share it with those around us. We are here to make much of God's name. So how about it? Are we intentionally living to see others find Christ as Savior?

Closing Benediction: "May we live fearlessly since God has

sealed us with the Holy Spirit. And may we live the life God has called us to on earth until we go to heaven. A life that helps others find Jesus. Amen."

DAY 37

"Israel"

Revelation 7:4-8

If you paid attention in geography class, you'd know Israel is a very small country. In fact, if you were to walk its length from north to south, it would only take a couple of days. Yet, this small country has had huge importance and impact in the world. Empires have fought over it. In fact, I recently read that every forty-four years out of the last four thousand, on average, an army has marched through it to either rescue or conquer it.

Luxembourg is about the same size geographically as Israel. Actually, it's a little bigger. But how often do you hear about Luxembourg in the news? Israel, however, is a country talked about on the world stage all of the time. Why is that? What makes Israel so important? Well, partly, it's because of its archaeological and historical sites. But, most importantly, Christianity originated in Israel. The Messiah was born in Bethlehem and died on a cross in Jerusalem. Israel is the land God gave to Abraham, the father of the Jewish people.

Israel was God's chosen people in the Old Testament, and I believe they are still God's chosen people. Those of us who are not Jewish, known as Gentiles, have the incredible opportunity to be part of God's chosen people, too. Romans 11 tells us Gentiles will be "grafted in" and considered part of God's "branches." Sadly, many Jews have not embraced Jesus as Messiah, but the Tribulation will be a period in which many Jews finally come to receive Jesus as their Lord and Savior. Take a look at Revelation 6:4-8:

And I heard the number of the sealed, 144,000, sealed from every tribe of the sons of Israel: 12,000 from the tribe of Judah were sealed, 12,000 from the tribe of Reuben, 12,000 from the tribe of Gad, 12,000 from the tribe of Asher, 12,000 from the tribe of Naphtali, 12,000 from the tribe of Manasseh, 12,000 from the tribe of Simeon, 12,000 from the tribe of Levi, 12,000 from the tribe of Issachar, 12,000 from the tribe of Zebulun, 12,000 from the tribe of Joseph, 12,000 from the tribe of Benjamin were sealed.

The twelve tribes of Israel come from the twelve sons of Jacob, whose name was changed to Israel, according to Genesis. Jacob was the son of Isaac, who was the son of Abraham. It was through Abraham that God chose to birth a nation that would be His chosen people. These 144,000 Jews represent God's hand on His chosen people, even amidst the judgment of Israel refusing to embrace Jesus as Messiah. From each tribe, God would spare their lives and use them to help reach their fellow Jews.

Part of the reason for the Tribulation is to purge the nation of Israel as a time for the Jews to finally bow a knee to Jesus. The 144,000 is a reminder God does not give up on His people. Even amidst judgment, there is grace. God is faithful, even when we sometimes are faithless. I hope that's a source of encouragement to you today. We serve a covenant-keeping, faithful God.

Closing Benediction: "May we be thankful we have a God who remains faithful even when we aren't. May His faithfulness challenge us to be faithful in our relationship with Him. Amen."

DAY 38

"The Unreached Reached"

Revelation 7:9-12

There are approximately 17,400 different people groups, of which around 7,400 are considered unreached. There are 7.8 billion people on the earth, and 3.3 billion of them are unreached. According to the Joshua Project, unreached people groups are those in which there is no indigenous community of believing Christians with adequate numbers and resources to evangelize their people.[17] In my opinion, churches need to focus much of their missionary energies on these particular groups.

When Jesus was getting ready to leave the earth, He gave His disciples the following instructions in Matthew 28:19, "Go therefore and make disciples of all nations." Jesus wants us to reach every corner of the world with the gospel. Even though the Tribulation will be a time of incredible pain and punishment, it will also be a time of increased gospel activity. Look at Revelation 6:9-12:

After this, I looked, and behold, a great multitude that no one could number, from every nation, from all tribes and peoples and languages, standing before the throne and before the Lamb, clothed in white robes, with palm branches in their hands, and crying out with a loud voice, "Salvation belongs

> *to our God who sits on the throne, and to the Lamb!" And all the angels were standing around the throne and around the elders and the four living creatures, and they fell on their faces before the throne and worshiped God, saying, "Amen! Blessing and glory and wisdom and thanksgiving and honor and power and might be to our God forever and ever! Amen."*

When most people think of the Tribulation, they think of judgment, not redemption. However, in the vision John receives, people will come to know Christ from "every nation, from all tribes and peoples and languages." What an absolutely amazing vision! There will not be an area of the world that the gospel won't penetrate. Having said that, it doesn't negate the church's responsibility now to seek to reach every nation, tribe, and people with the gospel of Jesus Christ.

In today's passage, it says we will all worship before the throne along with the angels, the heavenly elders, and four living creatures. It will be glorious as every group of people gathers together as one. Why would we not want to reach others on Earth to be part of this heavenly family? And yet, how often do we live to build our own castles made of sand instead of giving ourselves to our heavenly home, whose foundation is built on the Lamb of God?

The Church must rise and get serious about the mission Jesus has left us with, to "go therefore and make disciples of all nations." Let us not give ourselves to lesser things. We are part of something so much bigger than ourselves—So much bigger than our church programs and church politics. We are part of something so big it demands our all.

Closing Benediction: "May the Church rise and live out its calling to reach every tribe and nation. May each of us individually see our daily activities as opportunities to make disciples. Amen."

DAY 39

"Mercy Amidst Judgment"

Revelation 7:13-14

In his book *Experiencing God's Forgiveness*, Luis Palau tells the story of a mother who once approached Napoleon seeking a pardon for her son. Napoleon replied that the young man had committed the offense twice, and justice demanded death. But the woman explained, "I don't ask for justice, I plead for mercy."

Napoleon replied, "But your son does not deserve mercy."

"Sir," the woman cried, "it would not be mercy if he deserved it, and mercy is all I ask for."

To which Napoleon replied, "Well then, I will have mercy." And he spared the woman's son from death.[18]

Amid judgment for sin in the Tribulation, there will also be many examples of mercy. Many will be given an opportunity to turn to Christ, even though they had rejected Him before the Tribulation began. The Tribulation is a reminder that in the midst of judgment, God offers mercy. Look at Revelation 7:13-14:

> *Then one of the elders addressed me, saying, "Who are these, clothed in white robes, and from where have they come?" I said to him, "Sir, you know." And he said to me,*

"These are the ones coming out of the great tribulation. They have washed their robes and made them white in the blood of the Lamb."

We must have a balanced view of who God is. God is a Righteous Judge, so He punishes sin. But God is also a Gracious Father, so He offers His mercy, grace, and forgiveness to those who repent. It's true now, and it will be true in the Tribulation as well. All of this is made possible because One died for all. Psalm 85:10 says, "Mercy and truth have met together; righteousness and peace have kissed."

It's at the cross that "mercy and truth" meet and "righteousness and peace" kiss. Righteousness and truth are fulfilled because God said the price for sin was death, and Jesus became that death. Mercy and peace were made available because someone else covered the cost on our behalf. We are sinners and deserve death, but Jesus became that death. His victory on the cross ensured our victory over death. It ensured our place in glory.

Those converted during the Tribulation stand before God in His glory because "they have washed their robes and made them white in the blood of the Lamb." And that's our story, too— the blood of the Lamb has washed us. One day, we will bow with all the saints of old. We will join Paul and Peter, Mary and Martha, Moses and Elijah, and David and Esther. We will join our loved ones who knew Jesus but have passed from this earth, and in one accord, we will worship the Lamb . . . the Lamb that shed His blood on our behalf.

Closing Benediction: "May we live each day with a thankful heart that God has demonstrated His mercy and truth in our lives. And has given us everything we need to live a righteous life of peace. Amen."

DAY 40

"Cannonballs In the Sky?"

Revelation 7:15-17

In the country music video "Outskirts of Heaven" by Craig Campbell, kids share their perspective of what Heaven will be like. One girl says, "The sky is going to be pink, and the birds are going to be blue." A little boy describes it as being "magical, with lots of gold and cloud houses. Oh, and squishy." Another boy shared that he hopes his cat Meow-Meow and his dog Rocky will be there. And another kid shares confidently that Heaven "will have a bunch of toys and a remote control helicopter." Another shares his plans in Heaven, saying, "I'll be jumping on the clouds and doing cannonballs in the sky."

Cute video, if not exactly theologically accurate. One of the most asked questions in Christianity is, "What will Heaven be like?" Some of the answers to our questions about Heaven won't be answered until we get there. However, the book of Revelation does at least give us a glimpse of what glory will be like. In today's passage, we see martyred Christians from the Tribulation in Heaven. This description helps us understand a little bit more about Heaven. Look at Revelation 7:15-17:

> *Therefore they are before the throne of God, and serve him day and night in his temple; and he who sits on the throne will shelter them with his presence. They shall*

hunger no more, neither thirst anymore; the sun shall not strike them, nor any scorching heat. For the Lamb in the midst of the throne will be their shepherd, and he will guide them to springs of living water, and God will wipe away every tear from their eyes.

From this passage, we learn some things about Heaven: #1 We will serve God there. #2 We will experience His presence at all times. #3 We will never hunger or thirst again. #4 We will never get burned by the sun. #5 We will never shed tears of pain. That sounds pretty good, doesn't it? Even better than doing cannonballs in the sky!

This passage only gives us a glimpse of heaven, but what a glorious glimpse it is. We will serve God in His presence and never thirst or hunger for more. We will be fully satisfied. No more pain and no tears. It's important to remember our future when the present isn't going well. We need to remember that it's momentary in light of eternity. We must remember, nothing can take our inheritance away. We are sealed as saints of the living Savior. Rejoice in that today despite the circumstances you may be facing. And who knows, maybe we will do cannonballs in the sky!

Closing Benediction: "May we rejoice in the future return of Christ. May it encourage us no matter what we might face today. May we choose to smile today because God has prepared a glorious future for us. Amen."

DAY 41

"Bowl Of Prayers"

Revelation 8:1-5

Early believers in a particular area of Africa were known for their passion for prayer. Each of them had a separate spot in the thicket for their time with God. Over time, the paths to these places would become worn down. If one of these believers began to neglect their prayer life, it would become apparent to others. They would remind the individual neglecting prayer, "The grass grows on your path."

What about us? Have we allowed the grass to grow on our path? Or are we passionate in prayer? E.M. Bounds was a godly man from the 1800's who wrote eleven books, nine of them about prayer. He said the following: "What the Church needs today is not more machinery or better, not new organizations or more novel methods, but men whom the Holy Ghost can use—men of prayer, men mighty in prayer."[19]

Of course, it's not just men but also women who need to be mighty in prayer. One of the reasons we lose our passion for prayer is that we don't always see the results. Perhaps we sometimes wonder if our prayers are making any difference at all. Well, today's passage answers that question for us. Look at Revelation 8:1-5:

When the Lamb opened the seventh seal, there was silence in heaven for about half an hour. Then I saw the seven angels who stand before God, and seven trumpets were given to them. And another angel came and stood at the altar with a golden censer, and he was given much incense to offer with the prayers of all the saints on the golden altar before the throne, and the smoke of the incense, with the prayers of the saints, rose before God from the hand of the angel. Then the angel took the censer and filled it with fire from the altar and threw it on the earth, and there were peals of thunder, rumblings, flashes of lightning, and an earthquake.

This isn't the first mention of "the prayers of all the saints" being kept in Heaven in golden bowels. We first see this vision in chapter five as well. Before God unleashes a new set of Tribulation judgments, known as the Trumpet Judgments, God reveals the bowl of prayers to John.

It's important to remember that Revelation was written to be a source of comfort to John, and the churches who were facing persecution. And one of the areas of encouragement to the saints is the bowl of prayers. How so? Because the bowl is a reminder God heard their prayers, holds on to our prayers, and uses them for His eternal plans. Remember that the next time you feel like giving up on prayer.

Closing Benediction: "May we never forget how important our prayers are to God and His plans. May we be passionate prayer warriors in this world as we seek to live for a better world God has for us. Amen."

DAY 42

"Eagle Cry"

Revelation 8:6-13

Some people cry a lot, and some rarely do. My kids make fun of me because I shed tears easily. I've been known to cry at Hallmark commercials. I probably get teary-eyed on a monthly basis when I preach. It's just the way I'm wired, I guess.

Now, I'm not a crybaby. I think that's a whole other thing. A crybaby is a complainer. Someone who's too sensitive. Someone wimpy. No, my tears are more the result of being tenderhearted. I cry when the pain of others moves me. I cry when I'm just so proud of my wife or kids. I cry when I become overwhelmed by the grace of God in my life.

I think some things are worth crying over. In today's passage, we look at the first four Trumpet Judgments. These Tribulation judgments are enough to bring tears to the eyes. And they do. Not to a human, but to a bird. Yep, a bird. Take a look at Revelation 8:6-13:

Now the seven angels who had the seven trumpets prepared to blow them. The first angel blew his trumpet, and there followed hail and fire, mixed with blood, and these were thrown upon the earth. And a third of the earth was burned up, and a third of the trees were burned up, and all green grass was burned up. The second angel blew his trumpet, and something like a great mountain, burning with fire, was thrown into the sea, and a third of the sea became blood. A third of the living creatures in the sea died, and a third of the ships were destroyed. The third angel blew his trumpet, and a great star fell from heaven, blazing like a torch, and it fell on a third of the rivers and on the springs of water. The name of the star is Wormwood. A third of the waters became wormwood, and many people died from the water, because it had been made bitter. The fourth angel blew his trumpet, and a third of the sun was struck, and a third of the moon, and a third of the stars, so that a third of their light might be darkened, and a third of the day might be kept from shining, and likewise a third of the night. Then I looked, and I heard an eagle crying with a loud voice as it flew directly overhead, "Woe, woe, woe to those who dwell on the earth, at the blasts of the other trumpets that the three angels are about to blow!"

There's much here to process, but I will just summarize these first four judgments. Judgment #1 will be hail, fire, and blood destroying one-third of the earth's vegetation. Judgment #2 will be a burning mountain, and one-third of the sea will become blood, killing one-third of the sea creatures. Judgment #3 will be stars falling from the sky and one-third of the drinking water becoming contaminated. Lastly, judgment #4 will be heavenly bodies colliding and one-third of the Earth's light being lost.

Stop and think about all of that for a moment. The lives that will be ruined. The economic collapse, and so much more, yet the next couple of judgments will be even worse. That causes this heavenly eagle to cry, "Woe, woe, woe."

The reality of a coming judgment for those who don't know Christ should move us to tears. Do our hearts break for those far from God? Do our hearts break to the point of being intentional with gospel conversations? Do our hearts break to the point that we fall on our knees daily and cry out for God to save the unbelievers in our lives?

Closing Benediction: "May we weep for the lost. May we care so deeply for the souls of others that we pray deeply for them and have the courage to share our faith with them. Amen."

DAY 43

"Spooky Creatures"

Revelation 9:1-12

There seems to be an abundance of movies and TV shows that revolve around creatures from other planets. The popular Marvel movies have that theme in nearly all of their movies. A popular television show is *Stranger Things*, and it has two primary themes: the 80s and monsters.

I could go on and on naming movies and shows with aliens and monsters. Of course, these are fictional characters, but what if it wasn't as fictional as we thought? In today's passage, we see that monster-like creatures from another place will be part of the Tribulation judgments. Look at Revelation 9:1-12:

And the fifth angel blew his trumpet, and I saw a star fallen from heaven to earth, and he was given the key to the shaft of the bottomless pit. He opened the shaft of the bottomless pit, and from the shaft rose smoke like the smoke of a great furnace, and the sun and the air were darkened with the smoke from the shaft. Then from the smoke came locusts on the earth, and they were given power like the power of scorpions of the earth. They were told not to harm the grass of the earth or any green plant or any tree, but only those people who do not have the seal of God on their foreheads. They were allowed to torment them for five months, but not to kill them, and their torment was like the torment of a scorpion when it stings someone. And in those days people will seek death and will not find it. They will long to die, but death will flee from them. In appearance the locusts were like horses prepared for battle: on their heads were what looked like crowns of gold; their faces were like human faces, their hair like women's hair, and their teeth like lions' teeth; they had breastplates like breastplates of iron, and the noise of their wings was like the noise of many chariots with horses rushing into battle. They have tails and stings like scorpions, and their power to hurt people for five months is in their tails. They have as king over them the angel of the bottomless pit. His name in Hebrew is Abaddon, and in Greek he is called Apollyon. The first woe has passed; behold, two woes are still to come.

What a horrific account. These demonic beings will inflict so much pain on people that they will try to take their own lives, yet they won't be able to. By the way, the Hebrew word "Abaddon" and the Greek word "Apollyon" mean destroyer. There is a destroyer over these creatures. Because he's from the abyss, it's probably not Satan but one of his chief lieutenants.

So often, it's easy to forget about the warfare going on in the spiritual realm. Paul tells us in Ephesians 6:11-12, "Put on the whole armor of God, that you may be able to stand against the schemes of the devil. For we do not wrestle against flesh and blood, but against the rulers, against the authorities, against the cosmic powers over this present darkness, against the spiritual forces of evil in the heavenly places."

There's a whole Satanic army seeking to destroy the kingdom of God, and it's also true during the time of the Tribulation. But for those of us who know Christ, we have nothing to fear. Jesus triumphed over the Evil One at the grave, and someday, He'll cast that evil loser into the Lake of Fire! Let's live with confidence and courage, since we're on the winning side.

Closing Benediction: "May we never live in fear when we see evil all around us. May we live like the conquerors we are. Conquerors in Christ! Amen."

DAY 44

"Death"

Revelation 9:13-19

There have been hundreds and hundreds of wars since the beginning of civilization. World War I and World War II were two of the deadliest wars of all time. World War I lasted from 1914 to 1918. Eighteen million people died in the war; eleven million were in the military, and seven million were civilians.

World War II lasted from 1939 until 1945. It was the deadliest war in history, killing over seventy million people. Known for its genocidal campaign against the Jews, the war was responsible for the deaths of more than fifty million civilians. These two wars, which happened within a span of thirty-one years, saw the deaths of almost ninety million people.

As tragic as that was, today's passage tells us about a war that will be far more costly. Look at Revelation 9:13-19:

Then the sixth angel blew his trumpet, and I heard a voice from the four horns of the golden altar before God, saying to the sixth angel who had the trumpet, "Release the four angels who are bound at the great river Euphrates." So the four angels, who had been prepared for the hour, the day, the month, and the year, were released to kill a third of mankind. The number of mounted troops was twice ten thousand times ten thousand; I heard their number. And this is how I saw the horses in my vision and those who rode them: they wore breastplates the color of fire and of sapphire and of sulfur, and the heads of the horses were like lions' heads, and fire and smoke and sulfur came out of their mouths. By these three plagues a third of mankind was killed, by the fire and smoke and sulfur coming out of their mouth. For the power of the horses is in their mouths and in their tails, for their tails are like serpents with heads, and by means of them they wound.

This war involves an angelic army of "twice ten thousand times ten thousand." That means two hundred million, and they unleash the fury of judgment on the land. The passage says that one-third of the population will be killed. Let's say that five billion people are alive when the Tribulation begins. In the first set of judgments, we learned that one-fourth of the population will be killed. That leaves 3.75 billion people. And then, in the second judgment, the war will take one-third of that population. So, this war will take the lives of 1.25 billion people.

If you put all of that together, the Seal and Trumpet Judgment will take the lives of about 2.5 billion individuals. I'll be honest, that's hard to digest. All the pain and the heartache. But let's not forget that God is a holy God, and the consequence for sin, when repentance and trust in Christ doesn't occur, is death. The consequence goes all the way back to the Garden of Eden.

But you might say, "But many who come to know Christ during the Tribulation will also die." Yes, this is true, but isn't death a good thing for the follower of Christ? Death is the beginning of true eternal life. We, as believers, must get back to a Biblical understanding of life and death. We must recapture an eternal perspective, and we must remember just how holy God is and just how great an offense our sin is. Still, in the midst of it all, God extends His grace time and time again.

Closing Benediction: "May we remember that it's only by God's grace that death is not the end of our story. May the realities of the consequences of sin motivate us to share the hope of Christ with others. Amen."

DAY 45

"A Change Of Fortunes"
Revelation 9:20-21

There once was a man who had all the world could offer. Money, possessions, prestige. He wore the finest clothes money could buy. He feasted sumptuously every day. There was another man who lived in the same town. He lived on the streets. His meals were whatever handouts he could find for the day. He was sickly and smelly.

He was the type of person that fine, upstanding people in society avoided. If they saw him on the side of the street, they would walk over to the other side of the street. This man was an annoyance to the rich man, and the rich man would throw his scraps to the beggar, as if he was one of his dogs.

Every time the poor man came begging, the rich man would think, "I am so glad I'm not like him. He has nothing, and I have everything this world has to offer." Then, one day, the rich man died. Shortly after, the poor beggar died. Only then did the rich man understand that having all the world has to offer means nothing in the afterlife. The rich man, who had everything, now had nothing, and the poor man, who had nothing, gained everything.

This story I told is not my own. I simply retold it. It is a story told by Jesus of Lazarus and the rich man, found in Luke 16. The story did not end where I left off. Jesus peels back the afterlife and allows us to see Lazarus in Paradise and the rich man in Hades.

The rich man saw Abraham with Lazarus by his side. The rich man was in torment and begged for a drop of water, asking Abraham to send Lazarus—the irony of it all. The rich man begs the poor man. But there would be no relief for the rich man, or should I say former rich man, for there was a chasm between both places so a person could not pass from one to the other.

Then, the man thought of all his brothers on earth. They had to be warned to repent of sin and turn to Christ or else this would be their fate as well, so he begged Abraham to send Lazarus to preach the gospel to them. But Abraham told the man that if they didn't respond to the Scriptures, they wouldn't respond to Lazarus coming back from the dead.

Think about that, friends. Even someone coming back from the dead won't be enough to change the sinful hearts of some. That's how depraved the human heart is without Christ. This reality will play out during the Tribulation as well. Despite the judgments for sin, many will still refuse to bow a knee to Christ. Look at Revelation 9:20-21:

The rest of mankind, who were not killed by these plagues, did not repent of the works of their hands nor give up worshiping demons and idols of gold and silver and bronze

*and stone and wood, which cannot see or hear or walk,
nor did they repent of their murders or their sorceries
or their sexual immorality or their thefts.*

It may be easy to read this passage and conclude that it's pointless to pray for unbelievers or share our faith with them since the heart is so stubborn. It's true about the heart and that Jesus said more will not turn to Him than those who will. Yet, still, many will, and we don't know who those are. But we have the power of prayer and the power of the Word of God as we share Christ, and through the Holy Spirit, it can break through the most rebellious heart.

Our hearts need to break for the lost to the point that it causes us to pray and pray often for their souls, and it should motivate us to get out of our comfort zone and share the hope of Jesus with them.

Closing Benediction: "May our hearts break for broken people. May we pray hard and pray often for those in need of Jesus. And may we share the hope of Christ with those God places in our lives. Amen."

DAY 46

"Fighting Angels"
Revelation 10:1-7

It's interesting to see all the different opinions about angels. Some see them as our loved ones watching over us. Some see them as chubby babies with wings playing harps on the clouds. Others see them as beings who come back in human form to help others so they can earn their wings back.

Of course, none of these accurately depict who angels really are. These views come more from Hollywood rather than the Holy Scriptures. Movies like *It's a Wonderful Life* and the 90s TV show *Touched by an Angel* were entertaining, but not exactly Biblically accurate.

We may not know everything angels do, but we have enough Scripture to know a lot of what they do. Angels worship God and protect His throne. Angels deliver messages from God. Angels also minister to believers, though there's not a lot of Scripture given on what that looks like.

Angels are mentioned over sixty times in the Book of Revelation. We see in the Book that they play an important role in the unfolding of future events. Angels will help bring about the establishment of God's kingdom for eternity. In Revelation 10, we see a mighty angel mentioned. Look at vs. 1-7:

Then I saw another mighty angel coming down from heaven, wrapped in a cloud, with a rainbow over his head, and his face was like the sun, and his legs like pillars of fire. He had a little scroll open in his hand. And he set his right foot on the sea, and his left foot on the land, and called out with a loud voice, like a lion roaring. When he called out, the seven thunders sounded. And when the seven thunders had sounded, I was about to write, but I heard a voice from heaven saying, "Seal up what the seven thunders have said, and do not write it down." And the angel whom I saw standing on the sea and on the land raised his right hand to heaven and swore by him who lives forever and ever, who created heaven and what is in it, the earth and what is in it, and the sea and what is in it, that there would be no more delay, but that in the days of the trumpet call to be sounded by the seventh angel, the mystery of God would be fulfilled, just as he announced to his servants the prophets.

We don't know a lot about this mighty angel. Some have suggested that it was Jesus coming in the form of an angel, which I don't think is the case, though his depiction could represent the Triune God. The clouds represent God the Father, and the rainbows are a reminder of His covenant promise to mankind. The sun represents God the Son, and the fire represents God the Spirit.

Angels are mysterious creatures in many ways, but we know they not only fight for God's glory, they fight for us believers as well. When you read Revelation, you see angels as an army battling evil. The book of Daniel reveals the angel Michael coming to Daniel's aid after having fought with an angel from Persia.

In 2 Kings 6, the servant of Elisha had his eyes opened, and he could see a whole army of angels ready for battle. I don't know what spiritual battles between God's angels and Satan's angels look like, but there is great comfort in knowing that we have angels, too many to count, fighting on our behalf. What a challenge it is to make sure we're doing our part to fight the good fight of faith.

Closing Benediction: "May we be in awe of all God has done to ensure our victory. May we take time to remember the angels fighting for us. May it motivate us to give our all for the Kingdom of God. Amen."

DAY 47

"Seafood Diet"

Revelation 10:8-11

I remember my grandma having a quote on her kitchen wall: "I'm on a seafood diet. When I see food, I eat it." Unfortunately, I live by that diet way too often! The key to a healthy food diet is to eat balanced meals. If we only eat what we like, we'd mainly eat dessert. While that would be fun, it would also be unhealthy.

A balanced diet is the key to health, and a balanced diet of God's Word is the key to spiritual health. In today's passage, John is given the words of God. But oddly, he is told to eat it. Why? I have no idea. Take a look at Revelation 10:8-11:

Then the voice that I had heard from heaven spoke to me again, saying, "Go, take the scroll that is open in the hand of the angel who is standing on the sea and on the land." So I went to the angel and told him to give me the little scroll. And he said to me, "Take and eat it; it will make your stomach bitter, but in your mouth it will be sweet as honey." And I took the little scroll from the hand of the angel and ate it. It was sweet as honey in my mouth, but when I had eaten it my stomach was made bitter. And I was told, "You must again prophesy about many peoples and nations and languages and kings."

This is such an interesting passage of Scripture. John receives revelation from God, but is told not to share it and to actually eat the scroll that the words came on. Let's be honest, there are some passages in Revelation where you just shrug your shoulders and accept the fact that we probably won't understand it until we get to Heaven.

But there is something in this passage I want us to think about. The words from God were both sweet and bitter. I think that can also be said of the Bible. It is sweet to the soul, filled with sweet promises from God, but there are portions of it that are bitter and hard to digest, because it involves judgment and even death for sin. Remember, we need a balanced diet of God's Word.

We should not selectively read parts of the Bible we enjoy. We must read the whole counsel of God's Word. Why? So that we will become spiritually healthy. I won't be healthy eating desserts all day. I need to eat my vegetables, my peas, and green beans. They may not taste as good, but they lead to better health.

Don't neglect challenging passages of Scripture. They will help you grow. Remember, God had a reason for including it. Do I always enjoy reading Leviticus or Numbers? Not really. But I trust God, and I trust He has a reason for me to read it. God has not called us to stay as "babes." He wants us to grow into maturity.

Hebrews 5:13-14 says, "...for everyone who lives on milk is

unskilled in the word of righteousness, since he is a child. But solid food is for the mature."

Closing Benediction: "May we feast on the wonderful Word of God. May we taste and see that the Lord is good. May we commit our lives to the whole counsel of God's Word. Amen."

DAY 48

"The Power Of A Life Lived Well"

Revelation 11:1-6

Never underestimate the power of a life well lived. I am convinced when we get to Heaven, we will realize the eternal impact godly moms have had in the lives of their children and grandchildren through the powerful testimony of a daily walk with God. Or the mark of the faithful Sunday School teacher who, year after year, poured his or her heart and soul into teaching and loving kids. There is great power in our witness.

In fact, if you look at the surveys that have been done on how people come to a saving knowledge of Jesus Christ, the number one reason isn't the pastor giving an altar call or some big outreach event at church. The number one reason is the influence of a believer in their life. Never underestimate the power of a life lived well.

In Revelation 11, we are introduced to a couple of Tribulation figures. They are simply called the "two witnesses." Look at vs. 1-6:

Then I was given a measuring rod like a staff, and I was told, "Rise and measure the temple of God and the altar and those who worship there, but do not measure the court outside the temple; leave that out, for it is given over to the nations, and they will trample the holy city for forty-two months. And I will grant authority to my two witnesses, and they will prophesy for 1,260 days, clothed in sackcloth." These are the two olive trees and the two lampstands that stand before the Lord of the earth. And if anyone would harm them, fire pours from their mouth and consumes their foes. If anyone would harm them, this is how he is doomed to be killed. They have the power to shut the sky, that no rain may fall during the days of their prophesying, and they have power over the waters to turn them into blood and to strike the earth with every kind of plague, as often as they desire.

In the vision John receives, the identity of the two witnesses is not revealed. Based on the descriptions given, when combined with some Old Testament passages, many believe them to be Moses and Elijah, returning to the earth to proclaim the gospel. Amid worldwide persecution of believers, and in particular, Jewish believers, they will lead many to Christ.

Whoever these two witnesses are, they will have miraculous power, and their witness will impact many lives. It may not look the same for us today, but there is power in our witness as well. God's power is activated when we embody the gospel with our lives.

Romans 1:16 says, "For I am not ashamed of the gospel, for it is the power of God for salvation to everyone who believes, to the Jew first and also to the Greek." There is power in the gospel. There is power in a life changed by the gospel.

I've been a pastor for over thirty years. People have always appreciated my teaching of God's Word, but when I look over the many years in ministry with my wife and family, most people don't remember the sermons I've preached. It has been the relationship with them, and trying to model what living for Christ looks like in real life, that has impacted their lives.

You don't have to preach to many people to impact lives for the Kingdom of God. There's power in your witness. Live and share the gospel and see what God does.

Closing Benediction: "May we live daily a life that reflects Jesus. May we never give up trying to reach those far from God. May we never underestimate the power of living the gospel to those around us. Amen."

DAY 49

"Comeback Story"

Revelation 11:7-14

Everyone loves a good comeback story—whether it's a person down on their luck and their fortunes change or a team who makes a miraculous comeback in the fourth quarter. We love to celebrate these redemptive type stories.

Our family likes to watch *America's Got Talent*. People from all over the country perform their unique talents, and a panel of judges determines who makes it through the rounds until a champion is declared. The winner gets 1 million dollars and their own Las Vegas show.

I love to see unique and unusual talents. I once saw a young lady do a talent show with trained chickens and roosters. You don't see that every day. But my favorite part is when someone who has experienced some tragedy or has struggled with some disease or handicap, and then see they shine on the show and watch the crowd embrace them. It's moving. Why? Because everyone loves a good comeback story.

You could say that the gospel is the greatest example of a comeback story. Our sin has left this world and our lives a mess, yet God sends His Son to die for our sins. Then, He triumphs over the grave to ensure our victory over sin and death.

It truly is the ultimate comeback story.

Throughout Scripture, we see different individuals in desperate situations who embrace God, leading to redemption in their lives—individuals like Moses and David and Esther and Ruth. In today's passage, we see the two witnesses killed as the world rejoices over their demise, but their story is a miraculous comeback story. Look at Revelation 11:7-14:

And when they have finished their testimony, the beast that rises from the bottomless pit will make war on them and conquer them and kill them, and their dead bodies will lie in the street of the great city that symbolically is called Sodom and Egypt, where their Lord was crucified. For three and a half days some from the peoples and tribes and languages and nations will gaze at their dead bodies and refuse to let them be placed in a tomb, and those who dwell on the earth will rejoice over them and make merry and exchange presents, because these two prophets had been a torment to those who dwell on the earth. But after three and a half days, a breath of life from God entered them, and they stood up on their feet, and great fear fell on those who saw them. Then they heard a loud voice from heaven saying to them, "Come up here!" And they went up to heaven in a cloud, and their enemies watched them. And at that hour there was a great earthquake, and a tenth of the city fell. Seven thousand people were killed in the earthquake, and the rest were terrified and gave glory to the God of heaven. The second woe has passed; behold, the third woe is soon to come.

From death to life. From defeat to victory. God will ultimately receive the glory as these two witnesses will defeat the enemies of God by defeating death. Perhaps our story isn't as spectacular as these two witnesses, but it's miraculous nonetheless when we embrace the gospel of Jesus Christ.

We, too, will someday rise from the grave and defeat the grips of death. While we're still on Earth, we can think about what God has healed and forgiven us from because of the work of His Son, Jesus Christ. If you've embraced the gospel, you are part of a long line of comeback stories. We are on the winning team, even if it doesn't always look like it. The good guys win, the bad guys lose. That's how the story ends.

Closing Benediction: "May we never forget there is victory in Jesus. May we be encouraged to know that even in the difficult seasons of life, our story will end in victory. Amen."

DAY 50

"The Ark Of The Covenant"
Revelation 11:15-19

There have been many archaeological discoveries over the years, but the Ark of the Covenant has eluded archaeologists throughout the centuries. The Ark has significant meaning to the people of God. It represents the dwelling place of God for the Old Testament Jews. The high priests would enter the holy of holies where the Ark of the Covenant dwelled. It was there that sacrifices were made for the sins of the people.

The Ark of the Covenant consisted of a pure gold-covered wooden chest with a lid called the mercy seat. Inside the Ark were the two stone tablets of the Ten Commandments, Aaron's rod, and a pot of manna from the years the Israelites wandered in the desert.

Searching for the remains of the Ark of the Covenant has been an obsession for many. The idea of discovering the Ark led to a very successful movie called *Raiders of the Lost Ark*, with Indiana Jones seeking this lost treasure.

Well, I want to let you in on a little secret—the Ark of the Covenant isn't lost at all. It's in God's possession and will make an appearance at the end of days. Look at Revelation 11:15–19:

> *Then the seventh angel blew his trumpet, and there were loud voices in heaven, saying, "The kingdom of the world has become the kingdom of our Lord and of his Christ, and he shall reign forever and ever." And the twenty-four elders who sit on their thrones before God fell on their faces and worshiped God, saying, "We give thanks to you, Lord God Almighty, who is and who was, for you have taken your great power and begun to reign. The nations raged, but your wrath came, and the time for the dead to be judged, and for rewarding your servants, the prophets and saints, and those who fear your name, both small and great, and for destroying the destroyers of the earth." Then God's temple in heaven was opened, and the ark of his covenant was seen within his temple. There were flashes of lightning, rumblings, peals of thunder, an earthquake, and heavy hail.*

One day, Jesus will return and truly reign over this world. When the Tribulation ends, He will return with the angels and the saints and establish the Millennial Kingdom, which will usher in the eternal state of Heaven or hell. Then, the Ark of the Covenant will be revealed. The Ark represents the presence of God. It represents the promises of God to keep His covenant relationship with His people. In the Old Testament, the one possessing the Ark experienced victory over their enemies.

One day, all wrongs will be made right, and the righteous will serve the Savior forever. The Ark of the Covenant is a reminder that God dwells with His people, resulting in victory. I personally believe no one will discover the Ark until God chooses to reveal it at the End Times. We don't need the Ark of the

Covenant here and now; we don't need to have a high priest go into the Ark and sprinkle blood on it. Jesus is our high priest, and He sprinkled His blood for our sins on the cross. The result is God's constant presence in our lives and the power that goes with it.

Closing Benediction: "May we be encouraged today as we are reminded we have the presence of God with us, and we have the power of God available to us. May we take time to celebrate our eternal victory in Jesus Christ. Amen."

DAY 51

"Satan Is A Loser"

Revelation 12:1-6

The demonic world has left more than a few people with the creeps. Horror movies have helped reinforce people's greatest fears about these evil spirit beings. While there certainly is demonic activity in our world today, it appears there will be an increase during the end days, and it will manifest itself in visible ways. Take a look at Revelation 12:1-6:

And a great sign appeared in heaven: a woman clothed with the sun, with the moon under her feet, and on her head a crown of twelve stars. She was pregnant and was crying out in birth pains and the agony of giving birth. And another sign appeared in heaven: behold, a great red dragon, with seven heads and ten horns, and on his heads seven diadems. His tail swept down a third of the stars of heaven and cast them to the earth. And the dragon stood before the woman who was about to give birth, so that when she bore her child he might devour it. She gave birth to a male child, one who is to rule all the nations with a rod of iron, but her child was caught up to God and to his throne, and the woman fled into the wilderness, where she has a place prepared by God, in which she is to be nourished for 1,260 days.

Now, a lot is going on here. Let me break down the different characters mentioned here during the last three and a half years of the Tribulation. The woman refers to the nation Israel, the great red dragon represents Satan, and the child represents Jesus Christ. So, what in the world is going on here?

Well, it's a brief history of Satan trying to destroy God's chosen people, Israel, and His Son, Jesus. In verses 1-4, we see that one-third of all the angels joined Satan in his rebellion against God. Satan was likely the highest of all angels, the anointed cherub, the most beautiful of all of God's creations. Isaiah 14 and Ezekiel 28 give accounts of Satan's fall from Heaven.

When Jesus was ready to be born, Satan tried using King Herod to have Him killed, but as we know, he was unsuccessful. But verse 5 does say that the "child was caught up to God and to his throne," which means Jesus did die but defeated death and went to the Father. This passage says He will one day "rule all the nations."

Before all that happens, the nation Israel will have to go through intense persecution during the last three and a half years of the Tribulation, but they will come through it. What I want us to notice is that Satan fails, ultimately, at every attempt, and that's a great reminder, because when we encounter demonic activity, it can be unsettling.

Remember, Satan has no power over us, unless we give it to him. The power of God trumps the power of this world every time. Let's live in the victory Jesus secured for us when He defeated death.

Closing Benediction: "May we live fearlessly because Jesus has given us all the power we need to be victorious. May we not give Satan a foothold in our lives. Amen.

DAY 52

"Thrown Out"

Revelation 12:7-11

I hate to admit it, but growing up, I was a big fan of professional wrestling. When I was really little, I actually thought they were real fights. As I became a teenager, I realized they were staged fights, but nonetheless, I kept watching. One of my favorite parts was when one wrestler picked up another wrestler, lifted him over his shoulders, and threw him out of the ring.

While that is all pretend, the day is coming when Satan and his evil allies are going to experience a major defeat and be cast out of the heavenly realm. Let's read about it in Revelation 12:7-11:

Now war arose in heaven, Michael and his angels fighting against the dragon. And the dragon and his angels fought back, but he was defeated, and there was no longer any place for them in heaven. And the great dragon was thrown down, that ancient serpent, who is called the devil and Satan, the deceiver of the whole world—he was thrown down to the earth, and his angels were thrown down with him. And I heard a loud voice in heaven, saying, "Now the salvation and the power and the kingdom of our God and the authority of his Christ have come, for the accuser of our brothers has been thrown down, who accuses them day and night before our God. And they have conquered him by the blood of the Lamb and by the word of their testimony, for they loved not their lives even unto death."

Michael is the greatest of angels. He is the protector of Israel. There will be a major rumble in Heaven during the Tribulation. What's interesting is that Satan and the angels are in Heaven. We know from the book of Job that Satan is allowed access to God. Someday, when Satan and the angels are in Heaven, they will get a beat down and permanently expelled from it. They will no longer have access to God's presence, and, as we will learn later in Revelation, they will ultimately be cast into the Lake of Fire.

We've discussed in this series the prominent role angels will play in the end times, and the greatest of angels, Michael, will bring about this major victory. When you combine the previous verses and today's, you see that a lopsided battle exists. It's like a high school football team taking on the Super Bowl champs. It's no contest.

However, it doesn't feel that way now, does it? It seems, sometimes, like the bad are winning— the moral decay in the world, the decline in church attendance, the lack of spiritual revival in our land. But take comfort. The day is coming when there will be a blowout victory. Remember that when you're struggling with sin, when you see God's name being mocked, when you see ungodly behavior being celebrated. Even a losing team can have a good quarter. The game has been decided. We are part of the championship team. Rejoice in that today.

Closing Benediction: "May we not take spiritual warfare lightly. May we stop to celebrate that we are ensured a victorious future. Amen."

DAY 53

"Good News/Bad News"

Revelation 12:12-17

I'm sure you've heard of good news/bad news jokes. For instance, here's one: The doctor says to the patient, "I've got good news and bad news. The good news is that you have twenty-four hours to live." To which the patient replied, "How is that good news? What's the bad news?" The doctor replies, "The bad news is that I've been trying to call you since yesterday."

I know, pretty corny. The reality is, life is full of good news and bad news. In our passage today, there is good news, and there is bad news. Let's see what they are. Look at Revelation 12:12-17:

Therefore, rejoice, O heavens and you who dwell in them! But woe to you, O earth and sea, for the devil has come down to you in great wrath, because he knows that his time is short! And when the dragon saw that he had been thrown down to the earth, he pursued the woman who had given birth to the male child. But the woman was given the two wings of the great eagle so that she might fly from the serpent into the wilderness, to the place where she is to be nourished for a time, and times, and half a time. The serpent poured water like a river out of his mouth after the woman, to sweep her away with a flood. But the earth came to the help of the woman, and the earth opened its mouth and swallowed the river that the dragon had poured from his mouth. Then the dragon became furious with the woman and went off to make war on the rest of her offspring, on those who keep the commandments of God and hold to the testimony of Jesus. And he stood on the sand of the sea.

So, the good news is that Satan will be permanently cast out of the presence of God in Heaven forever, as we looked at before. The bad news is that when it happens, he's going to wreak havoc on God's people on Earth during the last half of the Tribulation; specifically, through the Antichrist, he is going to try and destroy the nation of Israel.

I think it's important to keep an eye on Israel. Israel is not a mighty nation in many ways, and as mentioned earlier, it's actually very small. Yet, they are still God's people and will become prominent at the end of days. Jesus came as a Jewish man from the tribe of Judah, so the Israelites are very important to God's plans. Praise God; many will be saved in the Tribulation and reign with Christ during the Millennial Kingdom.

Let's rejoice, as verse 12 says, because we've been grafted in and are part of God's redemptive plan. We have been chosen just like Israel. There's good news and bad news for Israel and us. The bad news is that we have a sin nature, so we will experience defeat sometimes. The good news is that our eternity has been sealed, and no one can rob us of our eternal home. Satan's time is numbered, and he will be trampled in the end.

So, let's put verse 12 into practice this week. Let's rejoice at the incredible future we have stored up for us.

Closing Benediction: "May we rejoice with the angels at our redemption. May we pray for the nation of Israel. And may we wait well, until the day our Savior makes all things new. Amen."

DAY 54

"Endurance Race"

Revelation 13:1-10

Call me crazy, but a "Bucket List" item for me is to run an ultra marathon. An ultra is basically any distance longer than a marathon. The most popular are the 50k, 50 mile, 100k, and 100 miler. My goal is to run the 50k and see how it goes, and if I actually survive, look at a longer distance. If you think I'm out of my mind, it's nothing compared to what Dean Karnazes has done.

From October 12th through 15th, 2005, Karnazes ran 350 miles across Northern California, without stopping. A year later, Dean ran fifty marathons in fifty states in fifty consecutive days. I don't even know how that's humanly possible. Obviously, to be an endurance runner, you must have a lot of physical and mental endurance and strength. Endurance is important in our spiritual race as well. Today's passage touches on endurance at the end of a vision of the Satan-empowered Antichrist. Look at Revelation 13:1-10:

And I saw a beast rising out of the sea, with ten horns and seven heads, with ten diadems on its horns and blasphemous names on its heads. And the beast that I saw was like a leopard; its feet were like a bear's, and its mouth was like a lion's mouth. And to it the dragon gave his power and his throne and great authority. One of its heads seemed to have a mortal wound, but its mortal wound was healed, and the whole earth marveled as they followed the beast. And they worshiped the dragon, for he had given his authority to the beast, and they worshiped the beast, saying, 'Who is like the beast, and who can fight against it?" And the beast was given a mouth uttering haughty and blasphemous words, and it was allowed to exercise authority for forty-two months. It opened its mouth to utter blasphemies against God, blaspheming his name and his dwelling, that is, those who dwell in heaven. Also it was allowed to make war on the saints and to conquer them. And authority was given it over every tribe and people and language and nation, and all who dwell on earth will worship it, everyone whose name has not been written before the foundation of the world in the book of life of the Lamb who was slain. If anyone has an ear, let him hear: If anyone is to be taken captive, to captivity he goes; if anyone is to be slain with the sword, with the sword must he be slain. Here is a call for the endurance and faith of the saints.

We learn a few things about the Antichrist, referred to in this passage as the beast of the sea. He gets his power from Satan, he has a mortal wound that he's healed from, and the world will worship him. He will blaspheme God and seek to destroy the people of God. And it's within that context that John writes, "Here is a call for the endurance and faith of the saints."

It's hard to imagine becoming a Christian during the Tribulation and facing all of the tragedies and persecutions that will take place. We are not Tribulation Christians, but we are also called to endure for Christ. Hebrews 12:1-2 says, "Therefore, since we are surrounded by so great a cloud of witnesses, let us also lay aside every weight, and sin which clings so closely, and let us run with endurance the race that is set before us, looking to Jesus, the founder and perfecter of our faith, who for the joy that was set before him endured the cross, despising the shame, and is seated at the right hand of the throne of God."

These verses remind us of a couple of things. First, we need to throw off excess baggage if we are going to run the race. There are things that aren't sin, but they still slow us down in our walk with Christ. This could be a hobby we become obsessed with or a relationship that is affecting us spiritually. The passage also says we must throw off sin that trips us up, and the author of Hebrews says we must keep our eyes on Jesus.

In other words, keep your eyes on the prize, and remember what He endured on our behalf. He endured the cross to pay the price for sin. Throw off the baggage and keep your eyes looking forward, and you will be able to endure the challenges of living for Christ in a world that's becoming more and more Christ-less.

Closing Benediction: "May we not fear a world that opposes our faith. May we throw off all that hinders, and may we keep our eyes focused each day on our precious Savior, Jesus Christ. Amen."

DAY 55

"Diabolical Duo"

Revelation 13:11-18

Everyone needs a right-hand man (or woman). The Lone Ranger had Tonto. Batman had Robin. Sonny had Cher. Simon had Garfunkel. Abbot had Costello. Bert had Ernie. Fred Astaire had Ginger Rogers, and Sherlock had Watson. We are better together. Ecclesiastes says that two are better than one.

However, sometimes, two together are worse when they're bad or evil. Bonnie had Clyde. King Ahab had Jezebel. The Joker had Harley Quinn. And as we learn from today's passage, the Antichrist had the false prophet. Look at Revelation 13:11-18:

Then I saw another beast rising out of the earth. It had two horns like a lamb and it spoke like a dragon. It exercises all the authority of the first beast in its presence, and makes the earth and its inhabitants worship the first beast, whose mortal wound was healed. It performs great signs, even making fire come down from heaven to earth in front of people, and by the signs that it is allowed to work in the presence of the beast it deceives those who dwell on earth, telling them to make an image for the beast that was wounded by the sword and yet lived. And it was allowed to give breath to the image of the beast, so that the image of the beast might even speak and might cause those who would not worship the image of the beast to be slain. Also it causes all, both small and great, both rich and poor, both free and slave, to be marked on the right hand or the forehead, so that no one can buy or sell unless he has the mark, that is, the name of the beast or the number of its name. This calls for wisdom: let the one who has understanding calculate the number of the beast, for it is the number of a man, and his number is 666.

The false prophet will be able to perform miracles, just like the Antichrist. These miraculous works will deceive people and cause them to worship the Antichrist. It will cause them to get the mark of the beast, a mark of loyalty to the Evil One. Many in the Tribulation will not take on the number 666 out of fear but out of allegiance to the Antichrist.

Really, it's not so much the diabolical duo as it is an unholy trinity. Satan is ultimately behind it all, and so this unholy trinity consists of Satan, the Antichrist, and the false prophet. They pack a punch to draw people away from God. The only answer, the only possible way of victory, is through the Holy Trinity—God the Father, God the Son, and God the Spirit. Our triune God has all the resources we need to fight off the evil enemy.

God the Father loves and protects His children, God the Son daily intercedes on our behalf, and God the Spirit dwells in us and guides us daily in the ways of Jesus. We have all the spiritual resources we need, but we must choose to daily yield to our Triune God. Prayer is a great resource for victory. The Father receives and answers our prayers, as the Son intercedes as High Priest, and the Holy Spirit guides us in how we pray.

What an amazing truth to have all persons of the Godhead, providing the power and protection we need to be victorious.

Closing Benediction: "May we surrender daily to our Triune God. May we be aware of the Evil One's attacks, and may we daily find our strength in our all-powerful God. Amen."

DAY 56

"A Heavenly Choice"

Revelation 14:1-11

Perhaps you've heard the phrase, "You are what you eat." Its origin comes from a quote in 1826 by the French lawyer Jean Anthelme Brillat-Savarin: "Dis-moi ce que tu manges, je te dirai ce que tu es."[20] The English translation is "Tell me what you eat, and I will tell you what you are." In other words, what we choose to take in determines our bodies' healthiness (or unhealthiness).

I'm on a nutrition plan, so this quote is fitting for me. What I like to eat is cake, chips, and ice cream. It may bring temporary pleasure, but the long-term effect is an unhealthy body, and potentially a premature death. Instead, I'm primarily eating fruits, vegetables, and healthy meats. While I miss the naughty food, the ultimate results will far outweigh the temporary pleasures of unhealthy food.

Every day, we have a choice of what we will take in. Will we choose to take in God's Word and worship the Savior? Or will we indulge in the things this world has to offer? You, indeed, are what you eat. It's also true you become like who you follow. In Revelation 14:1-11 we see a reminder of this:

Then I looked, and behold, on Mount Zion stood the Lamb,

and with him 144,000 who had his name and his Father's name written on their foreheads. And I heard a voice from heaven like the roar of many waters and like the sound of loud thunder. The voice I heard was like the sound of harpists playing on their harps, and they were singing a new song before the throne and before the four living creatures and before the elders. No one could learn that song except the 144,000 who had been redeemed from the earth. It is these who have not defiled themselves with women, for they are virgins. It is these who follow the Lamb wherever he goes. These have been redeemed from mankind as firstfruits for God and the Lamb, and in their mouth no lie was found, for they are blameless. Then I saw another angel flying directly overhead, with an eternal gospel to proclaim to those who dwell on earth, to every nation and tribe and language and people. And he said with a loud voice, "Fear God and give him glory, because the hour of his judgment has come, and worship him who made heaven and earth, the sea and the springs of water." Another angel, a second, followed, saying, "Fallen, fallen is Babylon the great, she who made all nations drink the wine of the passion of her sexual immorality." And another angel, a third, followed them, saying with a loud voice, "If anyone worships the beast and its image and receives a mark on his forehead or on his hand, he also will drink the wine of God's wrath, poured full strength into the cup of his anger, and he will be tormented with fire and sulfur in the presence of the holy angels and in the presence of the Lamb. And the smoke of their torment goes up forever and ever, and they have no rest, day or night, these worshipers of the beast and its image, and whoever receives the mark of its name.'"

In this passage, John sees a vision of what will happen during the Tribulation. The 144,000 praise God with the heavenly beings, and we also see God's grace at work by allowing the gospel to go out on earth "to every nation and tribe and language and people." Still, some choose to follow the beast (Antichrist), and it will be to their eternal destruction.

We become who we follow. Follow Christ, and we become like Christ, and our eternity becomes secured. Follow the "god of this world," and a person will become ungodly, with eternal torment becoming their destiny. We all know people who haven't placed their faith in Christ. We need to remember what will be the result. I try to think about the results before I choose my food. It would be good for us as Christ's followers to stop and think about what the results will be for people in our lives who don't choose Christ. May it motivate us to share Jesus's hope with them.

Closing Benediction: "May we make the daily decision to choose to take in God and His Word. May we be intentional in helping those far from God find salvation in the Savior. Amen."

DAY 57

"Sickle"

Revelation 14:12-20

For thousands of years, various cultures have had figures to represent death. One of the most common is the Grim Reaper—a skeletal figure, who is often shrouded in a dark, hooded robe and carrying a scythe to "reap" human souls. Whenever I see a picture of the Grim Reaper, it gives me the creeps. The creepiest part is the blade he's holding. The scythe is similar to a sickle. The difference is that the sickle has a more rounded blade.

The sickle is an agricultural tool used for harvesting or reaping crops. The sickle is prominent in today's passage. And it's not the Grim Reaper who's holding. It is the Savior. Look at Revelation 14:12-20:

Here is a call for the endurance of the saints, those who keep the commandments of God and their faith in Jesus. And I heard a voice from heaven saying, "Write this: Blessed are the dead who die in the Lord from now on."

"Blessed indeed,' says the Spirit, "that they may rest from their labors, for their deeds follow them!" Then I looked, and behold, a white cloud, and seated on the cloud one like a son of man, with a golden crown on his head, and a sharp

sickle in his hand. And another angel came out of the temple, calling with a loud voice to him who sat on the cloud, "Put in your sickle, and reap, for the hour to reap has come, for the harvest of the earth is fully ripe." So he who sat on the cloud swung his sickle across the earth, and the earth was reaped. Then another angel came out of the temple in heaven, and he too had a sharp sickle. And another angel came out from the altar, the angel who has authority over the fire, and he called with a loud voice to the one who had the sharp sickle, "Put in your sickle and gather the clusters from the vine of the earth, for its grapes are ripe." So the angel swung his sickle across the earth and gathered the grape harvest of the earth and threw it into the great winepress of the wrath of God. And the winepress was trodden outside the city, and blood flowed from the winepress, as high as a horse's bridle, for 1,600 stadia.

Different people have different images of Jesus. One popular painting has a picture of a gentle-looking Savior who is carrying a sheep on His shoulders. There are many images of Jesus washing the feet of His disciples. I've seen paintings of Jesus standing in the boat teaching a crowd of people, but an image I've not seen of Jesus is Him holding a sickle, ready to swing it upon the people on earth.

This image doesn't mesh with the view of Jesus many people have. The reality is, Jesus came as "meek and mild," but when He returns, He will come as a conquering king who will right the wrongs done on the earth. He will come and reap a harvest that will include the bloodshed of those opposed to God. In fact, verse 20 tells us there will be bloodshed at His return that will rise to the mane on a horse.

This passage is a reminder God does not take sin lightly. That rebellion against God will be dealt with. That God is a just God and will settle the score when Jesus returns. What a reminder for us when it seems like evil people are winning or when we see so much oppression in the world. As we looked at before, may it motivate us to share the hope of Jesus with others. Revelation should fan the flame of evangelism in us. That's why, on numerous occasions, I've emphasized the need to share the gospel.

Jesus is a merciful Savior, yet He is also a just God. We must embrace all of who Jesus is. We may come to Him as "a friend who sticks closer than a brother" (Proverbs 18:24), but we must also remember He will right wrongs and discipline for sin. Let us come freely to Jesus, but let us come in humility and reverence.

Closing Benediction: "May we have a balanced view of our Savior. May we rejoice in His mercy and grace, but may we also take His justice and holiness seriously. Amen."

DAY 58

"Worship Is A Way Of Life"

Revelation 15:1-8

Johann Sebastian Bach wrote, "All music should have no other end and aim than the glory of God and the soul's refreshment; where this is not remembered, there is no real music but only a devilish hub-bub."[21] Bach headed all of his compositions with "J.J." They were the initials for "Jesus Juva," which means "Jesus helps me." He then ended his compositions with "S.D.G." These are the initials for "Soli Dei Gratia," meaning "To God alone be the glory."

It's not just music. Anything we do can and should be for God's glory. When it is, it's an act of worship. God has called us to a life of worship. A.W. Tozer gives an excellent description of worship: "What is worship? Worship is to feel in your heart and express in some appropriate manner a humbling but delightful sense of admiring awe and astonished wonder and overpowering love in the presence of that most ancient Mystery, that Majesty which philosophers call the First Cause, but which we call Our Father Which Are in Heaven."[22]

Would a life of worship describe us? Do we have that humbling, delightful sense of admiring awe and wonder and overpowering love for the Savior? I sure hope so, because we will worship the King for all eternity. Look at Revelation 15:1-8:

Then I saw another sign in heaven, great and amazing, seven angels with seven plagues, which are the last, for with them the wrath of God is finished. And I saw what appeared to be a sea of glass mingled with fire—and also those who had conquered the beast and its image and the number of its name, standing beside the sea of glass with harps of God in their hands. And they sing the song of Moses, the servant of God, and the song of the Lamb, saying, "Great and amazing are your deeds, O Lord God the Almighty! Just and true are your ways, O King of the nations! Who will not fear, O Lord, and glorify your name? For you alone are holy. All nations will come and worship you, for your righteous acts have been revealed." After this I looked, and the sanctuary of the tent of witness in heaven was opened, and out of the sanctuary came the seven angels with the seven plagues, clothed in pure, bright linen, with golden sashes around their chests. And one of the four living creatures gave to the seven angels seven golden bowls full of the wrath of God who lives forever and ever, and the sanctuary was filled with smoke from the glory of God and from his power, and no one could enter the sanctuary until the seven plagues of the seven angels were finished.

In this vision of the Tribulation, a powerful worship service is going on. There are so many reasons to worship God. This passage gives the following reasons: Because God is just and true in all His deeds and because He is holy and righteous in all He does. Will you take some time this week to meditate on God's deeds—His holiness, justness, and truthfulness?

Worship not only expresses our gratitude to God, but it also changes our own hearts and helps us find joy, even amid painful seasons of life. Psalm 103:1-2 says, "Bless the Lord, O my soul, and all that is within me, bless his holy name! Bless the Lord, O my soul, and forget not all his benefits." Let's not forget all His benefits to us. With all that we are and have, let us lift up the holy name of God.

Closing Benediction: "May we not get so consumed with the day-to-day of life that we forget to praise God's name today. May we take time to meditate on all the reasons we have to lift up holy hands in praise. Amen."

DAY 59

"Here Comes The Judge"

Revelation 16:1-11

I'm sure you've heard the phrase, "Here comes the judge." But do you know where it comes from? It originated from the soul and comedy singer Pigmeat Markham. And in case you were wondering, Pigmeat is a nickname. My guess is many of you haven't heard of Pigmeat Markham, but it's said he was the forerunner for rap music.

He wrote the song "Here Comes The Judge" in 1968. When famous singer and comedian Sammy Davis Jr. performed the song, it became a cultural phenomenon, which is why people are familiar with the term today. In reality, there truly will be a day when... "Here comes the judge." And that judge will be Jesus. The Tribulation is a powerful reminder that sinfulness will be judged. There will be a reckoning for the sin and evil of the world. We are reminded of this in today's passage, Revelation 16:1-11:

Then I heard a loud voice from the temple telling the seven angels, "Go and pour out on the earth the seven bowls of the wrath of God." So the first angel went and poured out his bowl on the earth, and harmful and painful sores came upon the people who bore the mark of the beast and worshiped its image. The second angel poured out his bowl into the sea, and it became like the blood of a corpse, and every living thing died that was in the sea. The third angel poured out his bowl into the rivers and the springs of water, and they became blood. And I heard the angel in charge of the waters say, "Just are you, O Holy One, who is and who was, for you brought these judgments. For they have shed the blood of saints and prophets, and you have given them blood to drink. It is what they deserve!" And I heard the altar saying, "Yes, Lord God the Almighty, true and just are your judgments!" The fourth angel poured out his bowl on the sun, and it was allowed to scorch people with fire. They were scorched by the fierce heat, and they cursed the name of God who had power over these plagues. They did not repent and give him glory. The fifth angel poured out his bowl on the throne of the beast, and its kingdom was plunged into darkness. People gnawed their tongues in anguish and cursed the God of heaven for their pain and sores. They did not repent of their deeds.

While it can be hard to hear of such tormenting judgment coming upon the earth, we must remember just how much of an offense sin is to a holy God. It is only by God's grace and the shedding of Jesus's blood that we are not all rightly wiped off the face of the planet. When we see God's judgment on display, it should cause all of us to fall to our knees in worship for God's mercy and forgiveness.

The judgment of God reminds us of His justice and that He is true to His word to right all wrongs. The justice and judgment of God give boundaries for our lives. They provide value to our pain and suffering. They give motivation for how we should live our lives. They remind us we need to share our faith with those who don't yet know Christ, and they give an example for us to follow. We are to be people of justice.

Here comes the Judge. May we never forget that, and may it make us the most humble and grateful people, knowing we will not be judged as sinners but as God's beloved children.

Closing Benediction: "May we fall and worship at the feet of the Righteous Judge. May we never forget our God is a God of justice. Amen."

DAY 60

"The War Already Won"
Revelation 16:12-21

Isn't it important to know what's worth fighting for and what isn't? Some of the wars over the years could be considered "Just Wars," as St. Augustine put it. But some of them were wars not worth fighting for. Some of them were downright ridiculous.

For instance, "The War of the Oaken Bucket" in 1325 between two states in Italy. This war began when a rivalry between Modena and Bologna spiraled out of control over . . . a wooden bucket. The trouble started when a band of Modena soldiers raided Bologna and stole a large wooden bucket.

The raid was successful, but Bologna declared war on Modena, wishing to secure both its bucket and its pride. The war raged on for twelve whole years, but Bologna never did manage to get its bucket back. To this day, the bucket is still stored in Modena's bell tower.

As we all know, it's not just in wars that we sometimes fight for things we shouldn't fight for. I saw on the news a fight that broke out at the Meteor Buffet in Huntsville, Alabama. The police were called, and arrests were made. What was the fight over? Crab legs. Someone budged in line for the crab legs. I like crab legs as much as the next person, but some things are worth fighting for, and others are not.

There will be a great war someday, and it's a war that must be fought. It's been ordained since the Garden. We learn about it in today's passage. Revelation 16:12-21:

> *The sixth angel poured out his bowl on the great river Euphrates, and its water was dried up, to prepare the way for the kings from the east. And I saw, coming out of the mouth of the dragon and out of the mouth of the beast and out of the mouth of the false prophet, three unclean spirits like frogs. For they are demonic spirits, performing signs, who go abroad to the kings of the whole world, to assemble them for battle on the great day of God the Almighty. ('Behold, I am coming like a thief! Blessed is the one who stays awake, keeping his garments on, that he may not go about naked and be seen exposed!') And they assembled them at the place that in Hebrew is called Armageddon. The seventh angel poured out his bowl into the air, and a loud voice came out of the temple, from the throne, saying, "It is done!" And there were flashes of lightning, rumblings, peals of thunder, and a great earthquake such as there had never been since man was on the earth, so great was that earthquake. The great city was split into three parts, and the cities of the nations fell, and God remembered Babylon the great, to make her drain the cup of the wine of the fury of his wrath. And every island fled away, and no mountains were to be found. And great hailstones, about one hundred pounds each, fell from heaven on people; and they cursed God for the*

plague of the hail, because the plague was so severe."

Now, a lot is going on in this passage, but what I want us to ultimately understand is that a final battle between good and evil, between Jesus and His archenemy Satan, is destined to occur. It will conclude the Tribulation, and usher in the Second Coming of Jesus and His reign on earth for all eternity.

As we will see in Revelation 19, we will join Jesus in this battle as part of His holy army, along with the angels, but we won't have to do much. Jesus will do it all, and we will reap the benefits of His defeat of Satan and his rebellious followers. This is a war we know we've already won, so let's live as victorious soldiers now.

Closing Benediction: "May we live in the confidence of being on the conquering side. May we follow after our Commander, Jesus Christ. Amen."

DAY 61

"The Man Who Fell Into A Hole"

Revelation 17:1-7

I heard a parable a couple of years ago about a man who fell into a hole. One passerby told the man he could be free of pain and suffering if he meditated long enough and reached nirvana. The man did his best to meditate but remained in the hole. Another person came across the man and told him to face the East, pray five times a day, and follow five tenants, and he'd be set free from his dilemma. Once again, the man in the hole did what he was told, but he still remained stuck.

Others came past the man in the hole and offered advice on what he should do to get out of the hole, but none of these things helped. When all hope seemed lost, a man appeared. This man lowered himself into the pit and took hold of the man. He brought him out of the hole and into the light, and the man was saved from sure death.

The point is Christianity does what all other religions cannot do. Christianity actually saves people. What separates Christianity from all other religions is that we believe it's what Jesus has done, not what we do, that brings salvation.

Karl Marx called religion "the opium of the people."[23] While there's hardly anything I'd agree on with Marx, this one I do. It seems like nearly everyone has some type of religion they feel they need—some "higher power" to look to.

Of course, as believers, we do have that "higher power," and His name is God. He is our Heavenly Father. In the end times, religion will be used to deceive the people, and it will actually keep them from the one true God. Look at Revelation 17:1-7:

Then one of the seven angels who had the seven bowls came and said to me, "Come, I will show you the judgment of the great prostitute who is seated on many waters, with whom the kings of the earth have committed sexual immorality, and with the wine of whose sexual immorality the dwellers on earth have become drunk." And he carried me away in the Spirit into a wilderness, and I saw a woman sitting on a scarlet beast that was full of blasphemous names, and it had seven heads and ten horns. The woman was arrayed in purple and scarlet, and adorned with gold and jewels and pearls, holding in her hand a golden cup full of abominations and the impurities of her sexual immorality. And on her forehead was written a name of mystery:

'Babylon the great, mother of prostitutes and of earth's abominations.' And I saw the woman, drunk with the blood of the saints, the blood of the martyrs of Jesus. When I saw her, I marveled greatly. But the angel said to me, "Why do you marvel? I will tell you the mystery of the woman, and of the beast with seven heads and ten horns that carries her."

There's a lot here—more than we can possibly explain. But, the "prostitute" is not literal Babylon. It's a metaphor to explain the one world order that the "beast," aka the Antichrist, sets up during the Tribulation, when he will use religion as a means of controlling the people. 2 Timothy 3:1 & 5 says, "But understand this, that in the last days there will come times of difficulty . . . having the appearance of godliness, but denying its power."

At the end of the Tribulation, it will all be revealed that the world religion of the Tribulation not only doesn't bring people to God, it also keeps them from God, which is exactly what the Anti-Christ wants. The Bible says that there are many "anti-christs" that exist today. They seem to be teaching good things, but, in actuality, they keep people from truly understanding their need for a Savior.

All of us have people in our lives who have a religion, but in reality, it's just "the appearance of godliness, but denying its power." Satan "masquerades as light" and oftentimes will use the appearance of good to keep people from God. We must embrace the gospel, and we must share the gospel with those around us. We never know the time left on earth. Like the parable I shared earlier, only Christianity has the answers that can save a life.

Closing Benediction: "May we embrace the truth of the gospel daily in our lives. May we fearlessly share the message of Jesus Christ with those around us. Amen."

DAY 62

"Conquering Lamb"

Revelation 17:8-18

As someone who has grown up playing and watching sports, I love competition. What I really love, however, is to watch an upset. It's one of the reasons I enjoy the NCAA Basketball Tournament, otherwise known as "March Madness." There always seem to be at least a couple of major upsets, with mid-major teams beating some teams from one of the major conferences.

We saw one of the biggest upsets just a few years ago. Saint Peter's was a No. 15 seed playing against a basketball dynasty, the Kentucky Wildcats, who were a No. 2 seed. They shocked the world when they beat Kentucky 85-79. But this "Cinderella" team was not done. They went on to win their next two games to become the first-ever No. 15 seed to make it to the Elite Eight.

From a human perspective, we have a major upset in today's passage of Scripture. At the end of the Tribulation, there will be a one world order, and the most powerful world leaders and nations will form an allegiance with the Antichrist against Israel and non-Jewish followers of Christ. It seems like it would be a total onslaught of God's people. Except for one thing . . . the star "player" is Jesus, and that changes everything. Look at

Revelation 17:8-18:

The beast that you saw was, and is not, and is about to rise from the bottomless pit and go to destruction. And the dwellers on earth whose names have not been written in the book of life from the foundation of the world will marvel to see the beast, because it was and is not and is to come. This calls for a mind with wisdom: the seven heads are seven mountains on which the woman is seated; they are also seven kings, five of whom have fallen, one is, the other has not yet come, and when he does come he must remain only a little while. As for the beast that was and is not, it is an eighth but it belongs to the seven, and it goes to destruction. And the ten horns that you saw are ten kings who have not yet received royal power, but they are to receive authority as kings for one hour, together with the beast. These are of one mind, and they hand over their power and authority to the beast. They will make war on the Lamb, and the Lamb will conquer them, for he is Lord of lords and King of kings, and those with him are called and chosen and faithful. And the angel said to me, "The waters that you saw, where the prostitute is seated, are peoples and multitudes and nations and languages. And the ten horns that you saw, they and the beast will hate the prostitute. They will make her desolate and naked, and devour her flesh and burn her up with fire, for God has put it into their hearts to carry out his purpose by being of one mind and handing over their royal power to the beast, until the words of God are fulfilled. And the woman that you saw is the great city that has dominion over the kings of the earth."

I would recommend underlining verse 14 in your Bible or write it on an index card and keep it with you. In fact, let's let that verse soak into our souls for a moment: "They will make war on the Lamb, and the Lamb will conquer them, for he is Lord of lords and King of kings, and those with him are called and chosen and faithful."

Jesus, the slaughtered sheep, who became the resurrected Savior, will one day return again and take out all enemies of God's people. Come on now; if that doesn't fire you up, I don't know what will! We worship the Lord of all lords, and the King of all kings. Let's live in that confidence today.

As I was walking this morning, I was listening to a worship song that reminded me that God is my champion, and because of that, the "giants" in my life will fall. Walking and singing, the song reminded me that I am crowned with confidence because I know the One who has conquered it all. Saints, that's who you are because of Whose you are!

As I was walking this morning, I was listening to worship music. One of the songs, "Champion" (Dante Bowe), really blessed my heart. The song talks about Jesus being the ultimate Champion, undefeated in every battle. And since we are seated in the Heavenly place, we are crowned with His confidence. Saints, that's who you are because of Whose you are!

Closing benediction: "May we never forget we serve the conquering Lamb. He is our champion, and with Him, we can live undefeated. Amen."

DAY 63

"A Trip To The Woodshed"

Revelation 18:1-8

A spanking. A paddling. A swat. A licking. A whooping. A trip to the woodshed. The dreaded spoon. There's controversy in our world today about whether you should spank a child or not. All I know is it certainly taught me respect for my parents and that there are consequences for bad actions.

If there are no consequences for wrong behavior, how will people learn? Hebrews 12 tells us that a loving father disciplines his children and that God, our Heavenly Father, will always discipline His children, whom He loves. But when it comes to the enemies of God, He won't bring a paddle; He'll bring the sword. God will not let the unholy go unpunished. Look at Revelation 18:1-8:

After this I saw another angel coming down from heaven, having great authority, and the earth was made bright with his glory. And he called out with a mighty voice, "Fallen, fallen is Babylon the great! She has become a dwelling place for demons, a haunt for every unclean spirit, a haunt for every unclean bird, a haunt for every unclean and detestable beast. For all nations have drunk the wine of the passion of her sexual immorality, and the kings of the earth have committed immorality with her, and the

> *merchants of the earth have grown rich from the power of her luxurious living." Then I heard another voice from heaven saying, "Come out of her, my people, lest you take part in her sins, lest you share in her plagues; for her sins are heaped high as heaven, and God has remembered her iniquities. Pay her back as she herself has paid back others, and repay her double for her deeds; mix a double portion for her in the cup she mixed. As she glorified herself and lived in luxury, so give her a like measure of torment and mourning, since in her heart she says, 'I sit as a queen, I am no widow, and mourning I shall never see.' For this reason her plagues will come in a single day, death and mourning and famine, and she will be burned up with fire; for mighty is the Lord God who has judged her."*

Notice that verse six says, "pay her back" and "repay her." Verse seven says, "give her a like measure of torment and mourning." And verse eight says, "for mighty is the Lord God who has judged her." As we saw the other day, the "she" is the one world order that arises during the Tribulation.

God will utterly destroy it. He will destroy the Antichrist behind it, and ultimately Satan, who's behind the Antichrist. The only one world order will be when God reigns on earth for eternity. God will not be mocked. He will rule from on high. Take comfort in your struggle with Satan. God will take him to the woodshed, and he won't be coming back!

Closing Benediction: "May we find comfort and strength in a mighty God who will judge the living and the dead. May we find courage in knowing that God will destroy the Evil One. Amen."

DAY 64

"Money Won't Matter"
Revelation 18:9-18

The Mega Millions lottery recently stood at 1.1 billion dollars. People think their lives would be great if they just won the lottery. It's the mistake people make in life . . . believing that money makes everything better.

King Solomon had more money than just about anyone. It's estimated that Solomon's net worth was somewhere around $100 billion today, yet this is what he wrote in Proverbs 23:4-5: "Do not wear yourself out to get rich; do not trust your own cleverness. Cast but a glance at riches, and they are gone, for they will surely sprout wings and fly off to the sky like an eagle."

Much like today, in the one world order, during the Tribulation, money and sex drive most everything. Yet, when Jesus comes in glory at His second coming, the world will discover that it's true about wealth, it will "sprout wings and fly off." Look at Revelation 18:9-18:

And the kings of the earth, who committed sexual immorality and lived in luxury with her, will weep and wail over her when they see the smoke of her burning. They will stand far off, in fear of her torment, and say, "Alas! Alas! You great city, you mighty city, Babylon! For in a single hour your judgment has come." And the merchants of the earth weep and mourn for her, since no one buys their cargo anymore, cargo of gold, silver, jewels, pearls, fine linen, purple cloth, silk, scarlet cloth, all kinds of scented wood, all kinds of articles of ivory, all kinds of articles of costly wood, bronze, iron and marble, cinnamon, spice, incense, myrrh, frankincense, wine, oil, fine flour, wheat, cattle and sheep, horses and chariots, and slaves, that is, human souls. "The fruit for which your soul longed has gone from you, and all your delicacies and your splendors are lost to you, never to be found again!" The merchants of these wares, who gained wealth from her, will stand far off, in fear of her torment, weeping and mourning aloud, "Alas, alas, for the great city that was clothed in fine linen, in purple and scarlet, adorned with gold, with jewels, and with pearls! For in a single hour all this wealth has been laid waste." And all shipmasters and seafaring men, sailors and all whose trade is on the sea, stood far off and cried out as they saw the smoke of her burning, "What city was like the great city?"

Money is never the answer. The Messiah is the only answer. He always has been and always will be. After the events of this chapter, He will reign on earth, and money will be the last thing on our minds. He will rule in righteousness, and we will have all we could ever need—and money won't be one of them.

Closing Benediction: "May we hold loosely to the things of this world. May we cling tightly to the Savior who will rule forever and ever. Amen."

DAY 65

"Blood For Blood"

Revelation 18:19-24

There are many issues Christians disagree on—issues such as drinking alcohol and dancing. Another one is capital punishment, otherwise known as the death penalty.

There are a few passages of Scripture that seem to condone capital punishment. In Genesis 9:6, God says, "Whoever sheds human blood, by humans shall their blood be shed; for in the image of God has God made mankind."

Another one is Romans 13:4, "For the one in authority is God's servant for your good. But if you do wrong, be afraid, for rulers do not bear the sword for no reason. They are God's servants, agents of wrath to bring punishment on the wrongdoer."

It would seem murder demands a heavy price. There are consequences for actions—blood for blood. When sin entered the world, as Satan tempted Adam and Eve, so did death. The fall of man brought bloodshed to the land. In fact, Adam and Eve's own son paid the price of a fallen world when Cain killed Abel.

It was only the blood of the Savior that brought redemption to mankind. As Hebrews 9:22 puts it, "without the shedding of blood there is no forgiveness of sins." The Tribulation will bring much bloodshed, but at the end of that, peace will come to the earth. Look at Revelation 18:19-24:

"And they threw dust on their heads as they wept and mourned, crying out, "Alas, alas, for the great city where all who had ships at sea grew rich by her wealth! For in a single hour she has been laid waste. Rejoice over her, O heaven, and you saints and apostles and prophets, for God has given judgment for you against her!" Then a mighty angel took up a stone like a great millstone and threw it into the sea, saying, "So will Babylon the great city be thrown down with violence, and will be found no more; and the sound of harpists and musicians, of flute players and trumpeters, will be heard in you no more, and a craftsman of any craft will be found in you no more, and the sound of the mill will be heard in you no more, and the light of a lamp will shine in you no more, and the voice of bridegroom and bride will be heard in you no more, for your merchants were the great ones of the earth, and all nations were deceived by your sorcery. And in her was found the blood of prophets and of saints, and of all who have been slain on earth."

Satan and his evil followers have shed the blood of countless numbers of Christ's followers over the years. The Tribulation will culminate with the blood of the believers avenged, and when the day ends, Jesus, our avenger, will rule in peace and purity.

There are no guarantees things will be fair on this side of heaven. The wrongs may not be fully righted on Earth, but that's what is so glorious about the end of days. Jesus and His people will triumph, and we will finally have a leader we can follow for all eternity.

Closing Benediction: "May we put our confidence in Christ today, knowing He will make all things right in His time. May we celebrate a God of justice. Amen."

DAY 66

"Heavenly Worship"
Revelation 19:1-5

There are so many different depictions people have about heaven. Many see Heaven as an eternity of just singing to Jesus. Now, I love to sing to the Lord, but there are other things I like to do. Having worked with men's ministries over the years, I know some guys simply don't like to sing publicly. I think there are those who have this picture of Heaven as just a worship service that lasts forever, and they kind of see Heaven as something that will be boring.

There is nothing about heaven that will be boring. We will do many things in heaven, not just sing songs to Jesus. Randy Alcorn, in his book *Heaven* gives us a great challenge about our thinking of heaven: "Nothing is more often misdiagnosed than our homesickness for Heaven. We think that what we want is sex, drugs, alcohol, a new job, a raise, a doctorate, a spouse, a large-screen television, a new car, a cabin in the woods, a condo in Hawaii. What we really want is the person we were made for, Jesus, and the place we were made for, Heaven. Nothing less can satisfy us."[24]

How true this quote is. Nothing will fully satisfy us except for the presence of Jesus in our lives, now and in Heaven. In the first five verses of Revelation 19, it's clear that when Jesus comes again, there will be great joy and great worship! Let's take a look:

> *After this I heard what seemed to be the loud voice of a great multitude in heaven, crying out, "Hallelujah! Salvation and glory and power belong to our God, for his judgments are true and just; for he has judged the great prostitute who corrupted the earth with her immorality, and has avenged on her the blood of his servants." Once more they cried out, "Hallelujah! The smoke from her goes up forever and ever." And the twenty-four elders and the four living creatures fell down and worshiped God who was seated on the throne, saying, "Amen. Hallelujah!" And from the throne came a voice saying, "Praise our God, all you his servants, you who fear him, small and great."*

Do our lives reflect passionate worship like these heavenly hosts do? Our God brings "salvation and glory and power," and that should cause us, every day, to pause and give Him praise. Because His judgments are always "true and just," we should come with great expectation on Sundays to lift high His name with our brothers and sisters in Christ.

Worship means worth-ship. It's any time we stop and give gratitude for how worthy God is to have our everything. Worship will be an exciting part of Heaven. But how about now? Do our lives reflect what glory will look like? Is your life marked with daily worship?

Closing Benediction: "May we prioritize worship of God in

our day-to-day lives. May we stop and reflect on all the ways our Savior is worthy of our praise. Amen."

DAY 67

"Best Wedding Ever"

Revelation 19:6-10

Becky and I have reached a fun stage in our parenting. Most of our kids are now adults. We love this stage and are blessed to have a great relationship with our adult kids. Shockingly, I think they like us and like being around us. Well, my wife, at least.

A year ago, the first of our kids was married. What a day full of joy. It was perfect weather. God was glorified in the ceremony. The reception was a great mixture of being sentimental and fun. It ranks up there as one of my favorite days I've had on this earth.

It's interesting what will happen at the conclusion of the Tribulation, a time marked by judgment and pain and death. There will be a joyful celebration. A celebration of a "groom," Jesus, with His "bride," the Church. The heavenly being in our passage today refers to it as "the marriage supper of the Lamb." Let's take a look. Revelation 19:6-10:

> *Then I heard what seemed to be the voice of a great multitude, like the roar of many waters and like the sound of mighty peals of thunder, crying out, "Hallelujah! For the Lord our God the Almighty reigns. Let us rejoice and exult*

and give him the glory, for the marriage of the Lamb has come, and his Bride has made herself ready; it was granted her to clothe herself with fine linen, bright and pure'— for the fine linen is the righteous deeds of the saints. And the angel said to me, 'Write this: Blessed are those who are invited to the marriage supper of the Lamb." And he said to me, "These are the true words of God." Then I fell down at his feet to worship him, but he said to me, "You must not do that! I am a fellow servant with you and your brothers who hold to the testimony of Jesus. Worship God.' For the testimony of Jesus is the spirit of prophecy."

Jewish weddings, during Bible times, were different than today. Even the engagement was different. Today, a person who gets engaged can call it off, if they want. In Bible times, an engagement was a legally binding agreement. Today, a wedding is a one-day ceremony, actually more like half a day. In Bible times, it was typically a seven-day celebration.

The celebration would begin with the groom and his friends going to the house of the bride with a torchlight parade through the streets. They would proceed to the groom's home, which would kick off celebrating days. What a great way to describe Jesus (the groom) ushering in life together on Earth with His followers (the bride).

I loved my son's wedding, but that won't even compare to the Savior's wedding we get to be a part of. The second coming of Jesus will be marked with joyful celebration. Why not get some practice in now? Let's live a joy-filled, celebratory life, as we await our King, our Groom.

Closing Benediction: "May we live joyful lives. May we take time to celebrate how great our God is each day. Amen."

DAY 68

"The Tale Of Two White Horses"
Revelation 19:11-13

Barry Bremen was an insurance salesman from Michigan. In the sports world, in the 1980s, he was known as "The Great Imposter." He posed as a Major League Baseball umpire in the World Series and as a player in the All-Star Game. He also pretended to be an NBA player in one of their All-Star Games and as a referee in the NFL. He even posed as a Dallas Cowboys cheerleader once!

He didn't limit it to sports, either. He crashed the 1985 Emmy Awards and accepted an award on stage that was supposed to go to a female actress. In a 1980 *People Magazine* profile, his wife, Margo, said that Barry was "fulfilling a grand fantasy to be in the limelight."[25]

It's amazing how far some people will go to get some glory. Satan was the most beautiful of angels, but he wanted glory, and it says in Ezekiel that he was cast out of Heaven because of it. In Ezekiel 28:16, God said to Satan: "…so I cast you as a profane thing from the mountain of God, and I destroyed you, O guardian cherub, from the midst of the stones of fire." But that didn't stop Satan. He has spent the rest of his pathetic life trying to trip up Christians and receive glory.

That's why he is going to send the Antichrist into the world during the Tribulation, to try to turn people to him instead of God. But the Antichrist is just a "poser." His time in the limelight will be limited. Revelation 6 says that he will come on a white horse and that he "had a bow, and a crown was given to him, and he came out conquering, and to conquer" (Revelation 6:2).

At the end of the Tribulation, when Christ returns, we see who the real leader on the white horse is. Look at Revelation 19:11-13:

Then I saw heaven opened, and behold, a white horse! The one sitting on it is called Faithful and True, and in righteousness he judges and makes war. His eyes are like a flame of fire, and on his head are many diadems, and he has a name written that no one knows but himself. He is clothed in a robe dipped in blood, and the name by which he is called is The Word of God.

Jesus is the "faithful and true" Savior, and it's not one crown; it's "many diadems," for He will rule the whole world, and every knee will bow before Him. Jesus wins. Satan loses. That's how the story ends. Let's live in that truth this week.

Closing Benediction: "May we live with a victorious spirit today. Our Savior has given us everything we need to live in obedience. Amen."

DAY 69

"Two Roads"

Revelation 19:14-18

In high school, we were required to memorize Robert Frost's poem, *The Road Not Taken*. Now, I was too busy trying to memorize the lines to actually stop and think about the meaning of the poem. And to be honest, I'm still not sure of the full meaning of it.

I still do, however, remember the following lines, "Two roads diverged in a wood, and I—I took the one less traveled by, and that has made all the difference."[26]

While I don't care enough about poetry to ponder the poem's meaning, I know that the Bible mentions two roads people must choose from. It's Jesus who talked about it, and I care deeply what the meaning of His words are.

These two roads Jesus discusses are found in Matthew 7:13-14: "Enter through the narrow gate. For wide is the gate and broad is the road that leads to destruction, and many enter through it. But small is the gate and narrow the road that leads to life, and only a few find it."

One road is broad, and many take it, but it leads to destruction. The other road is narrow, few take it, but it leads to life. I believe the two roads are the paths people will take in eternity. One is Heaven, and sadly, the other is hell.

At the Second Coming of Christ, we see that road also leads to a supper. One, the Marriage Supper of the Lamb. We looked at that already. In Revelation 19:14-18, we learn about the other supper. Take a look:

And the armies of heaven, arrayed in fine linen, white and pure, were following him on white horses. From his mouth comes a sharp sword with which to strike down the nations, and he will rule them with a rod of iron. He will tread the winepress of the fury of the wrath of God the Almighty. On his robe and on his thigh he has a name written, King of kings and Lord of lords. Then I saw an angel standing in the sun, and with a loud voice he called to all the birds that fly directly overhead, "Come, gather for the great supper of God, to eat the flesh of kings, the flesh of captains, the flesh of mighty men, the flesh of horses and their riders, and the flesh of all men, both free and slave, both small and great."

Those who refuse to choose Jesus will be devoured in this supper. It's the "great supper of God." One road leads to joyful feasting; the other road leads to the fury of God. Choose this day whom you will serve. Eternity is at stake.

Closing Benediction: "May we find joy and delight in the joyful feast that awaits us in heaven. May we pray diligently for people in our lives who are following the wrong road. Amen."

DAY 70

"Bullies"

Revelation 19:19-21

Some have experienced the pain and fear of being bullied when they were younger. I used to be bullied for being the shortest kid in class when I was in elementary school. I was bullied a little bit in ninth grade as well. Those experiences gave me a chip on my shoulder against people who bully.

That's why I enjoy superhero movies. It's essentially the bully getting what he or she deserves. Satan is the biggest bully of all, and he recruits the "diabolical duo," the Antichrist and the False Prophet, during the Tribulation to try to help him defeat Jesus and those who turn to Jesus.

But the conclusion of Revelation 19 is a great reminder he will fail in the end. Look at verses 19-21:

And I saw the beast and the kings of the earth with their armies gathered to make war against him who was sitting on the horse and against his army. And the beast was captured, and with it the false prophet who in its presence had done the signs by which he deceived those who had received the mark of the beast and those who worshiped its image. These two were thrown alive into the lake of fire that burns with sulfur. And the rest were slain by the sword that came from

*the mouth of him who was sitting on the horse,
and all the birds were gorged with their flesh.*

Now, we will learn Satan's fate in the next chapter, but in this chapter, we discover the final home of these losers is the Lake of Fire. Spoiler alert: Someone else will be joining them soon! God settles scores, and the end times are our reminder of that.

Feeling bullied by Satan recently? Fear not; our God fights our battles, and the evil one is no match for Him. 1 John 4:4 tells us: "Little children, you are from God and have overcome them, for he who is in you is greater than he who is in the world." Live in that truth today!

Closing Benediction: "May we never forget that God fights our battles. May we never forget how our story ends. It ends victoriously. Amen."

DAY 71

"Satan's Pit"

Revelation 20:1-3

We have all known individuals who change the room's environment when they're around—and I don't mean for the better. Maybe it's a weird uncle who makes things awkward at a family gathering or the angry fan at a game who yells loudly at the official. Perhaps it's the narcissistic friend who steers every direction back to themselves.

And once they're gone, the tension leaves the room. If you can't think of anyone like that, maybe you're that person! Just kidding. Some people make things better, and some make things worse. That's just the way it is.

The Millennial Kingdom will be amazing because of who's running it—Jesus. It will also be amazing because of who *won't* be there. Take a look at Revelation 20:1-3:

Then I saw an angel coming down from heaven, holding in his hand the key to the bottomless pit and a great chain. And he seized the dragon, that ancient serpent, who is the devil and Satan, and bound him for a thousand years, and threw him into the pit, and shut it and sealed it over him, so that he might not deceive the nations any longer, until the thousand years were ended. After that he must be released for a little while.

There are so many things that are going to be awesome about the thousand-year reign of Christ on the Earth. One of those things is that God will throw Satan into the pit. Stop and think how amazing life will be without the influence of Satan.

Now, if you believe in a rapture like I do, those of us who are believers will already have our resurrection bodies, and we will be sinless, so we wouldn't have to worry about him. But for those who survive the Tribulation, and generations of people born during the Millennium, they will have a sinful nature and would have been very much affected by Satan's presence.

What does this mean for us now as followers of Christ? We are to exhibit the qualities of the coming kingdom of Christ now. Even though we can't escape the presence of Satan now, we can live in a way that limits his influence in our lives.

James 4:7 says, "Submit yourselves therefore to God. Resist the devil, and he will flee from you." When we surrender daily to Jesus, and say no to Satan's temptations, he will flee from us. Satan only has authority in our lives if we give it to him. Don't give Satan a foothold. So today, let us exhibit the Kingdom of God, by submitting to the Lord and kicking Satan to the curb!

Closing Benediction: "May we live under the rule and reign of Jesus today. May we put boundaries in our lives to keep Satan out. Amen."

DAY 72

"House Of Cards"

Revelation 20:4-6

"House of cards" is an expression that can be traced back to 1645. It means a structure built on a shaky foundation that will collapse when one or more elements are removed.

I am absolutely terrible at building things with my hands. I know from experience what a "house of cards" looks like. But thankfully, my faith is built upon the Rock. Nothing the world throws at me can cause it to crumble.

Jesus talks about what will last and what will fall. In Matthew 7, He said that building upon the things of the world is like building something out of sand, but building upon Christ and His Word will withstand any storm. It's a firm foundation.

Many people are trying to build thrones for their own lives, but it's just a house of cards. In today's passage, we are reminded of the thrones that last. Look at Revelation 20:4-6:

Then I saw thrones, and seated on them were those to whom the authority to judge was committed. Also I saw the souls of those who had been beheaded for the testimony of Jesus and for the word of God, and those who had not worshiped the beast or its image and had not received its mark on their foreheads or their hands. They came to life and reigned with Christ for a thousand years. The rest of the dead did not come to life until the thousand years were ended. This is the first resurrection. Blessed and holy is the one who shares in the first resurrection! Over such the second death has no power, but they will be priests of God and of Christ, and they will reign with him for a thousand years.

In the Kingdom, there will be those of us who return with Christ and the Second Coming, the martyred saints of the Tribulation who will be resurrected, and individuals who survive the Tribulation. Old Testament saints may be resurrected at this point as well.

So, who are the ones who sit on "thrones?" I believe it is all believers in Christ. We all will have thrones of authority as we serve Christ in the Kingdom. I believe the twelve apostles will have a special place of authority, according to Matthew 19:28.

Not only will we sit on thrones, we will serve as "priests of God and of Christ," serving and reigning with Christ in the Kingdom. What a future God has in store for us. I hope that encourages you today, no matter what you may be facing in this life.

Closing Benediction: "May we give God glory today for providing such an amazing future for us because of Christ. May we let God reign, and may we serve Him faithfully in preparation for the coming Kingdom. Amen."

DAY 73

"The End"

Revelation 20:7-10

We grew up reading or hearing stories that began with "Once upon a time" and ended with simply "The end." The Bible is no different.

The "Once upon a time" is found in Genesis 1. It's a perfect God creating a perfect world with perfect people, and then a problem occurs. Sin entered the world, and the results were catastrophic. Deadly, you could say.

Enter the hero: Jesus, Savior of the world. He solved the sin problem when He was crucified on a cross and resurrected from the dead—a glimmer of hope pierced through this fallen, broken world. Heaven came down, and glory filled our souls!

One day, "the end" will occur, but it's really just the beginning. It's the end of sin. It's the end of Satan, and it's the beginning of life as it was meant to be. Look at Revelation 20:7-10:

And when the thousand years are ended, Satan will be released from his prison and will come out to deceive the nations that are at the four corners of the earth, Gog and Magog, to gather them for battle; their number is like the sand of the sea. And they marched up over the broad plain of the earth and surrounded the camp of the saints and the beloved city, but fire came down from heaven and consumed them, and the devil who had deceived them was thrown into the lake of fire and sulfur where the beast and the false prophet were, and they will be tormented day and night forever and ever.

If ever there was a one-sided match, this will be it. Satan will gather millions upon millions in one last rebellious attempt for the throne of heaven and earth. God will strike with heavenly fire, and the devil will be sent to his eternal home, the "lake of fire." The End.

Imagine a world with no sin in it. Imagine a world without the temptations of Satan. Imagine a world filled with nothing but perfection. That's how our story ends—a story that never really ends.

This is the gospel. Heaven is our "Once upon a time" in which we will never hear nor experience "The end." Celebrate the gospel story. Celebrate, because it's our story. The end.

Closing Benediction: "May we celebrate our redemption story today. May we find hope and comfort knowing that the enemy is a defeated foe. Amen."

DAY 74

"Book Of Life"
Revelation 20:11-12

Have you ever had to look on a list to see if your name was included? Perhaps you tried out for a musical at your school, and you had to see if you were given a part, and, if so, which part. Or perhaps you tried out for the basketball team and had to see if your name was on the roster and if you made the cut.

Growing up, I experienced the joys of seeing my name on the roster, but I've also experienced the pain of not seeing my name listed or called out. Acceptance and rejection are just realities of life. Sometimes you make it, and sometimes you don't. Sometimes you're good enough, and sometimes you aren't. That's just life.

But there is one list, a list above all lists, that you want to make sure your name is on. But this list isn't about whether or not you were good enough. It's about whether you believe or not. Let's take a look. Revelation 20:11-12:

Then I saw a great white throne and him who was seated on it. From his presence earth and sky fled away, and no place was found for them. And I saw the dead, great and small, standing before the throne, and books were opened. Then another book was opened, which is the book of life. And

> *the dead were judged by what was written in the books, according to what they had done.*

At the end of the Millennial Kingdom, a "great white throne" will appear, and there will be books at this throne. But one book will be the most important of all books. It will be "the book of life." If a name isn't in the book, it won't be a musical or a basketball team a person won't get to be on. It will be Heaven they won't be able to be a part of.

It says God will judge the unbeliever "according to what they had done." This doesn't mean good works get people into heaven or keep them out. The works are the proof of whether a person placed their faith in Jesus Christ or not.

The Book of Life is a reality and should lead us to answer two questions. Number one, "Is my name written in the Book of Life?" And number two, "Are there people in my life whose names are not written in the Book of Life?" The reality of this book should cause us to make sure we are saved through the blood of Christ, and it should motivate us to share the gospel of Jesus Christ with others.

Closing Benediction: "May we find assurance of our salvation. Father, please give us the power and strength to share Jesus with those around us. Thank you for such a great salvation. Amen."

DAY 75

"Over Our Dead Bodies"
Revelation 20:13-15

There is no more difficult doctrine to discuss than the doctrine of hell. What makes it so difficult is because it's not just a theological truth to talk about; it's real people, and potentially people we love, who may experience the realities of hell if they don't repent and place their faith in Jesus.

The great British preacher of the 1800s, Charles Spurgeon, once wrote: "Think lightly of hell, and you will think lightly of the cross. Think little of the sufferings of lost souls, and you will soon think little of the savior who delivers them."[27] We must not ignore the realities of hell. We must accept the whole counsel of God's Word.

If we don't stop and remind ourselves of the reality of hell, we will lack depth in our understanding and appreciation for who Christ is and what He has done for us at Golgotha. If we are to think much of our Savior, we must allow ourselves to be moved by a very real and literal place known as hell. Look at Revelation 20:13-15:

And the sea gave up the dead who were in it, Death and Hades gave up the dead who were in them, and they were judged, each one of them, according to what they

> *had done. Then Death and Hades were thrown into the lake of fire. This is the second death, the lake of fire. And if anyone's name was not found written in the book of life, he was thrown into the lake of fire.*

Perhaps there are no more sobering words in the Bible than verse 15. What should our response be to today's passage of Scripture? Well, let me give you two of them. First, it should cause us to worship a God who, in His holiness, has every right to cast us into hell because of our sinful rebellion. Yet He makes a way, through the death and resurrection of Jesus, for us to be saved from hell and brought into a joyful relationship with Him that will last for all eternity.

The realities of hell should also cause us to weep. Our hearts should break for those who, unless they embrace Christ, will spend eternity in the "lake of fire." Broken, lost people should break our hearts to the point of sharing the hope of Jesus Christ with those who do not yet know Him. Yes, I know this has been the application in several of these devotionals. And yes, that's intentional. Revelation should motivate us to share the gospel.

To quote Spurgeon again: "If sinners be damned, at least let them leap to hell over our dead bodies. And if they perish, let them perish with our arms wrapped around their knees. If hell must be filled, let it be filled in the teeth of our exertions, and let no one go unwarned or unprayed for."[28] Can we honestly say that's our response to the realities of hell?

Closing Benediction: "May our hearts break for the broken.

May we be so moved by the lost that we spend each day with gospel intentionality. Thank you for redeeming us through the shed blood of Jesus. Amen."

DAY 76

"The Prince"

Revelation 21:1-4

Danish theologian Soren Kierkegaard once told the parable of a prince looking for a young maiden to marry as his future queen. While riding his carriage through a poor section of the village, he saw a beautiful, young peasant girl who captivated his heart. He could have ordered her to marry him, but the prince wanted the young lady to fall in love with him just as he had fallen in love with her.

The heir to the throne chose to give up his position and live in the village, working as a carpenter, to win the maiden's hand. This way, if she chose to accept his proposal of marriage, he would know that it wasn't because of what he would give her; it would be because she fell in love with him.

God could have created us as robots, but instead, He created us with a free will—a heart that can choose or not choose to love Him and accept Jesus as Lord and Savior. When sin came into the world, God chose to come down and do something about it. As John 1:14 puts it, "the Word became flesh and dwelt among us." Jesus left the heavenly palace to live in a sin-stained world to rescue us from our spiritual poverty.

Christianity isn't about trying really hard to reach Heaven. It's heaven coming down and rescuing us. Jesus came down to pay for our sins, and one day, God will bring a "new heaven and new earth" down to us for all eternity. Look at Revelation 21:1-4:

> *Then I saw a new heaven and a new earth, for the first heaven and the first earth had passed away, and the sea was no more. And I saw the holy city, New Jerusalem, coming down out of heaven from God, prepared as a bride adorned for her husband. And I heard a loud voice from the throne saying, "Behold, the dwelling place of God is with man. He will dwell with them, and they will be his people, and God himself will be with them as their God. He will wipe away every tear from their eyes, and death shall be no more, neither shall there be mourning, nor crying, nor pain anymore, for the former things have passed away."*

How amazing Heaven will be. He will bring a new world and a new city, free of sin's curse—a place where God will dwell with us in all His glory—a place where every tear will be wiped away—a place where death is no more—a place where mourning will be replaced with eternal joy. Pain will be eliminated, and every single day will be as perfect as the day before.

Max Lucado wrote in his book *Come Thirsty*: "With Christ as your friend and heaven as your home, the day of death becomes sweeter than the day of birth."[29] What a sweet and glorious future we have before us.

Closing Benediction: "May we find great delight today knowing that heaven will be the end of sin and all its consequences. May we be grateful for the grace of our loving God. Amen."

DAY 77

"New"

Revelation 21:5-8

It's funny the different smells some people like. There are some smells that most everyone likes—for instance, the smell of roses or cookies baking in the oven. I think I have an odd sense of what smells good, or so I've been told. I love the smell of nail polish and gasoline. I love the smell of new shoes. Okay, I admit this is weird, but I love to smell the inside of shoes when I buy them. Give it a few weeks, and I definitely would not like the smell of the shoes anymore!

Whether it's new shoes, a new car, or a house, there is something we tend to enjoy about a new smell. New is typically better than old, so it makes sense. Today's passage is a reminder that what makes heaven such joyful bliss will be that it's totally and completely new. Look at Revelation 21:5-8:

And he who was seated on the throne said, "Behold, I am making all things new." Also he said, "Write this down, for these words are trustworthy and true." And he said to me, "It is done! I am the Alpha and the Omega, the beginning and the end. To the thirsty I will give from the spring of the water of life without payment. The one who conquers will have this heritage, and I will be his God and he will be my son. But as for the cowardly, the faithless, the detestable, as for murder-

ers, the sexually immoral, sorcerers, idolaters, and all liars, their portion will be in the lake that burns with fire and sulfur, which is the second death."

What an encouraging word from the Lord, "Behold, I am making all things new." The old self, beaten and battered by sin, will be no more. A body with all its aches and pains will be no more. Sinful people causing grief will be no more. Heaven is a brand new slate. No sin, no sinful people, no pain, no need to repent, no need to do better, no regret. Verse 7 says we have a heritage in Heaven. Heritage can be defined as "property to be inherited; a special possession; an allotted portion."

Now, I don't have millionaires for parents, nor does my wife. We are not banking on an earthly inheritance that will allow us to spend our final years living in luxury. Quite honestly, we couldn't care less. But this I know: because we've committed our lives to Christ, my wife and I, and our kids as well, have a heavenly inheritance, with riches nothing on Earth could compare to. When God makes all things new, we will receive our heavenly heritage, our glorious inheritance.

Closing Benediction: "May we not live for earthly riches. May we live with eternity in mind. May we find our joy in the heritage that awaits us. Amen."

DAY 78

"Ranch Names"
Revelation 21:9-14

I've always loved driving out in the country past ranches with wooden signs at the entrance with the name of their family ranch. I always thought it would be cool to do that. But considering we live in a subdivision on less than a half acre of land and have no cattle or horses, it would probably not look so cool. Not to mention, it probably violates some Homeowner's Association code.

If I ever were to win the lottery, I'd buy a ranch and have a cool-looking wood sign at the entrance with some name like "Winding River Ranch" or "Hidden Cove Ranch." A man can dream. But here's the deal: when the new holy city comes down after the Millennial Kingdom, entrance into the city will have a name written on it. Actually, it will have twenty-four names written on it. Look at Revelation 21:9-14:

Then came one of the seven angels who had the seven bowls full of the seven last plagues and spoke to me, saying, "Come, I will show you the Bride, the wife of the Lamb." And he carried me away in the Spirit to a great, high mountain, and showed me the holy city Jerusalem coming down out of heaven from God, having the glory of God, its radiance like a most rare jewel, like a jasper, clear as crystal.

> *It had a great, high wall, with twelve gates, and at the gates twelve angels, and on the gates the names of the twelve tribes of the sons of Israel were inscribed—on the east three gates, on the north three gates, on the south three gates, and on the west three gates. And the wall of the city had twelve foundations, and on them were the twelve names of the twelve apostles of the Lamb."*

This brilliant capital city of Heaven will have twelve gates with the names of the twelve tribes of Israel. This is significant because Israel is still God's chosen people, and they will be honored with the names of the original twelve tribes. The twelve foundations of the wall to the city will have the names of the twelve apostles. This is significant because they represent the New Covenant and the life we have as a result of the finished work of Christ.

I love that both the Old and New Covenant will be represented in Heaven. Not only with names on the holy city but also with the presence of both Old and New Covenant believers. How cool will that be, seeing Moses and King David and Ruth and Esther. Who knows, maybe one of them will be your neighbor! So many exciting things about heaven. One will be the presence of the Old and New Testament saints.

Closing Benediction: "May we truly get excited now for the glories of Heaven later. May we find delight in knowing we will be in the company of the heroes of the faith for all eternity. And most of all, may we be thankful that we will be in the presence of God Almighty. Amen."

DAY 79

"The Coolest City"

Revelation 21:15-21

What's the coolest city you've ever been to? That's hard for me to answer. I have been blessed to travel around the world both for ministry and pleasure. Cape Town, South Africa, would definitely be high on my list, as would Athens, Greece, and London, England. I love the beauty of the landscape in Cape Town. I love history, so of course, Athens was amazing. And London, well, I just love British accents.

Well, each of these cities are dim in comparison to the capital city that will be part of Heaven, the "New Jerusalem." The mammoth size, the unique shape, and the materials of the city will make it unlike anything we have ever seen before. We get a description of it in Revelation 21:15-21:

And the one who spoke with me had a measuring rod of gold to measure the city and its gates and walls. The city lies foursquare, its length the same as its width. And he measured the city with his rod, 12,000 stadia. Its length and width and height are equal. He also measured its wall, 144 cubits by human measurement, which is also an angel's measurement. The wall was built of jasper, while the city was pure gold, like clear glass. The foundations of the wall of the city were adorned with every kind of jewel. The first was jasper, the second sapphire, the third agate, the fourth emerald, the fifth onyx, the sixth carnelian, the seventh chrysolite, the eighth beryl, the ninth topaz, the tenth chrysoprase, the eleventh jacinth, the twelfth amethyst. And the twelve gates were twelve pearls, each of the gates made of a single pearl, and the street of the city was pure gold, like transparent glass.

This capital city will be made of precious stones. The walls of the city will be 216 feet thick and 1,500 miles high, and 1,500 miles on each side. That's 2.25 million square miles! For comparison's sake, the largest city in the world, square foot wise, is New York City. It's 4,669 square miles. The New Jerusalem will be 2.25 million square feet. It will be big enough to accommodate approximately 100,000 billion people.

The main street of the city will be made of such pure gold that it will be like transparent glass. Everything about this city will be beautiful. When we read Revelation 22, we will discover some other incredible things about the city.

So, the next time you hit a pothole with your car, see run-down buildings in your city, or experience the effects of living in a city with too high of pollen levels or dirty and polluted waters, remember that this too shall pass. One day, we will have an eternal city that is more beautiful than the human mind could even comprehend. A city free from any effect of sin. A heavenly city. A perfect city. Our future home . . . the city of God!

Closing Benediction: "May we not grow weary when we see the effects of sin on our land. May we look ahead to our glorious home with our glorious Savior, and may it bring a sense of expectation to our souls today. Amen."

DAY 80

"Evel Knievel"
Revelation 21:22-27

I grew up watching the exploits of American stunt performer Evel Knievel. Known for his wild outfits (and wild living), he attempted some of the most fantastic motorcycle jumps the world has ever seen. Most of his jumps were successful, but not all of them.

As a result, in his career, he suffered numerous concussions, a crushed pelvis and femur, and fractures to his hip, wrist, and ankles. In his lifetime, Knievel attempted over seventy-five motorcycle jumps.

Perhaps his most famous stunt was an attempt to jump over the fountains at Caesars Palace Hotel in Las Vegas. However, during the landing, he fractured his skull. It left him comatose for a month. So what would possess Evel Knievel to risk life and limb?

Well, the answer comes from his own words. He once said, "Bones Heal, Chicks Dig Scars, Pain is Temporary, Glory is Forever."[30] Knievel was partly right—there is a glory that is forever. But there's also glory that fades. Knievel got a lot of glory during his lifetime. In fact, I was a huge fan, and even had his action figure and motorcycle to prove it.

But that Evel Knievel action figure is long gone, and as an adult, I see Knievel for who he really was. Not a hero, but a self-promoter, whose time of fame has come and gone. He lived for personal glory. But he was wrong. That kind of glory doesn't last forever. In today's passage, we see a glory that does. Look at Revelation 21:22-27:

And I saw no temple in the city, for its temple is the Lord God the Almighty and the Lamb. And the city has no need of sun or moon to shine on it, for the glory of God gives it light, and its lamp is the Lamb. By its light will the nations walk, and the kings of the earth will bring their glory into it, and its gates will never be shut by day—and there will be no night there. They will bring into it the glory and the honor of the nations. But nothing unclean will ever enter it, nor anyone who does what is detestable or false, but only those who are written in the Lamb's book of life.

Heaven will be an eternity of seeing the glory of God. So magnificent will be His glory, that there will be no need of sun or moon, for His glory will light the holy city of heaven.

People who saw the veiled glory of God in the Bible were forever changed. Imagine Heaven, when we get to see His unveiled glory each and every day—a glory that truly does last forever.

Closing Benediction: "May we yearn for Your glory, God. May we live daily to bring You glory for all who You are and all that You do. Amen."

DAY 81

"Redo"

Revelation 22:1-5

Redo. Wouldn't you love to have a "redo button?" I know I would. How many times do we wish we could take back a hurtful or careless word or a silly action fueled by pride or jealousy?

Way back in the Garden of Eden, Adam and Eve had it all. They were perfect people, living in a perfect place, loving and serving a perfect God. And then they ate of the fruit. I'm sure they wished they could have had a redo. All of creation was placed under a curse because of their sinful rebellion.

The glorious gospel is a reminder that God, in His love, will allow for a redo. Redemption through the blood of Jesus was the price for the redo. Mankind and creation would get a redo. The Garden of Eden will be restored. Look at Revelation 22:1-5:

Then the angel showed me the river of the water of life, bright as crystal, flowing from the throne of God and of the Lamb through the middle of the street of the city; also, on either side of the river, the tree of life with its twelve kinds of fruit, yielding its fruit each month. The leaves of the tree were for the healing of the nations. No longer will there be anything accursed, but the throne of God and of the Lamb will be in it, and his servants will worship him. They will see his face, and his name will be on their foreheads. And night will be no more. They will need no light of lamp or sun, for the Lord God will be their light, and they will reign forever and ever.

Heaven will include some elements of the original perfect place, Eden: a river, the Tree of Life, and the presence of God. God will redo the paradise He intended for us.

It says in verse 3 that "no longer will there be anything accursed." Imagine that. The curse of sin was completely removed. What an amazing future we have. A return to a perfect place, as perfect people, loving and serving a perfect God. Thank God for Jesus Christ, who brought redemption. We don't need a "redo button." We have a redeemer.

Closing Benediction: "May we surrender all to Jesus, who redeemed us. May we live with gratitude for a God who will restore all things. Amen."

DAY 82

"Hearing Vs. Heeding"

Revelation 22:6-9

There's a difference between hearing and heeding. If you have children, you know this. Our kids may hear what we say, but it certainly doesn't mean they will heed what we say.

And let's be honest, we were the same as kids. We've all intentionally disregarded our parent's instructions. Maybe we forgot what they told us, or maybe we just didn't want to do it. Whatever the reason, hearing but not heeding is an act of disobedience.

In the book of Revelation, we have heard many amazing things about the future, but Jesus wants to ensure we don't just settle for hearing. He wants us to heed His words about the coming Kingdom of Heaven. Look at Revelation 22:6-9:

And he said to me, "These words are trustworthy and true. And the Lord, the God of the spirits of the prophets, has sent his angel to show his servants what must soon take place. And behold, I am coming soon. Blessed is the one who keeps the words of the prophecy of this book." I, John, am the one who heard and saw these things. And when I heard and saw them, I fell down to worship at the feet of the angel who showed them to me, but he said to me, "You must not do that! I am a fellow servant with you and your brothers the prophets, and with those who keep the words of this book. Worship God."

This passage says, "Blessed is the one who keeps the words of the prophecy of this book." It says to "keep the words in this book." It's not enough just to read or hear the words of Revelation. We are to keep them. In other words, heed them, not just hear them.

How are the realities of heaven later changing how you live now? Are you living with eternity in mind? Are you living like Jesus could return at any moment? Are you finding joy in daily meditating on our future home? Let us not just hear; let us heed the eternal words of the Lord.

Closing Benediction: "May we grab hold of these prophetic words, and may it change how we live today. May eternity give us a sense of kingdom urgency. Amen."

DAY 83

"Washed"

Revelation 22:10-15

I remember the first time one of our boys went to church camp. My wife packed six pairs of underwear. When he got home, my wife opened the suitcase to clean his clothes, and all six pairs were still neatly packed. He had worn the same pair of underwear all week!

If "cleanliness is next to godliness," this kid was of the devil! That's an interesting phrase, isn't it, "Cleanliness is next to godliness?" Many trace the origin of the saying to John Wesley, co-founder of the Methodist movement. Of course, today, many refer to it as physical cleanliness. But my guess is that he meant it in the moral, spiritual sense.

The book of Leviticus had many rituals for the Jewish people and for the priests when it came to cleanliness before entering the temple to meet with God. While the Old Covenant rituals no longer bind New Covenant Christians, there are still examples we are intended to learn from them.

Entering the presence of a holy, pure God should cause us to come before Him with a pure and clean heart, but how in the world can a sinful man enter the presence of a sinless, perfect God? A well-known hymn answers that question for us.

The hymn, "Are you washed in the blood?" ends with these words: "Lay aside the garments that are stained with sin, and be washed in the blood of the Lamb. There's a fountain flowing for the soul unclean, O be washed in the blood of the Lamb!"

Heaven will be the home for those who have been washed in the blood of the Lamb. Look at Revelation 22:10-15:

And he said to me, "Do not seal up the words of the prophecy of this book, for the time is near. Let the evildoer still do evil, and the filthy still be filthy, and the righteous still do right, and the holy still be holy. Behold, I am coming soon, bringing my recompense with me, to repay each one for what he has done. I am the Alpha and the Omega, the first and the last, the beginning and the end. Blessed are those who wash their robes, so that they may have the right to the tree of life and that they may enter the city by the gates. Outside are the dogs and sorcerers and the sexually immoral and murderers and idolaters, and everyone who loves and practices falsehood."

All will stand before God and give an account. Some will remain "outside" of Heaven, and some will get in. They will "have the right to the tree of life" and will enter the gates! Verse 14 tells us who gets in: "Blessed are those who wash their robes." Washed with what? The precious blood of our Lord Jesus Christ.

Isaiah 1:18 says, "Come now, let us reason together, says the LORD: though your sins are like scarlet, they shall be as white as snow; though they are red like crimson, they shall become like wool." Cleanliness is next to godliness, and cleanliness doesn't come from human effort . . . it comes from a Savior who died for us, and who rose to defeat sin and death.

Closing Benediction: "May we live humbly and gratefully for what Jesus has done for us. May we strive for holiness in response to our salvation. Amen."

DAY 84

"Come"

Revelation 22:16-17

We as Christians believe in heaven, but do we truly yearn for it? I remember when I was in college thinking, "Lord, I do want You to return, but can I get married first and have some kids?" Now, maybe that seems pretty innocent enough. Most people want to get married and have kids. Yet looking back, I wonder if I was clinging too tightly to Earthly pleasures instead of yearning for Heavenly bliss.

My guess is I'm not the only one who sometimes feels the tug to want to live a full life and experience all it has to offer before going to glory. But if we really get who Jesus is, and really understand how glorious eternity is, it wouldn't even be a temptation to want to live longer on Earth. Instead, we would proclaim like Paul in Philippians 1:21, "To live is Christ, to die is gain!" Let's look at Revelation 22:16-17:

> *"I, Jesus, have sent my angel to testify to you about these things for the churches. I am the root and the descendant of David, the bright morning star.' The Spirit and the Bride say, 'Come.' And let the one who hears say, 'Come.' And let the one who is thirsty come; let the one who desires take the water of life without price."*

Jesus is our "bright morning star." His appearance wasn't much to look at when He came in human form, but His glorified body will be brilliant. Heaven isn't about a place, it's about a person . . . the "root and descendent of David." The reason Paul was so willing to say, "To die is gain," was because he was captivated by the Person of Jesus Christ.

In verse 17 of Revelation 22, it says all of us who hear the prophecy, should respond by saying, "Come!" Com,e Lord Jesus come. Do you yearn for Jesus' return? Do you hold the things and people of this world with loose grips? If the answer is "no," it's time for a come to Jesus moment. May we yearn for Yahweh. Come, Lord Jesus, come.

Closing Benediction: "May we truly yearn for Yahweh. May God help us look upward as we loosen our grip on the things of this world. Come, Lord Jesus, come. Amen."

DAY 85

"Yearning For Home"
Revelation 22:18-21

It's a pity there are some "crazies" who have hijacked the book of Revelation. You know who I'm talking about. The ones with wacky charts that somehow prove when Jesus will return or who the Antichrist is (typically a left-wing Democrat leader). These are the ones who love to put bumper stickers on their vehicles that say, "Warning: In case of Rapture, this car will be unmanned." They actually see this as a form of evangelism. If this is you, stop being weird! Mean and weird Christians make sharing the gospel harder for us fairly normal people.

My point is that Revelation has become one of those odd and hard-to-understand books for people, and so they stay away, which is a shame because God gave us the book to comfort us and not confuse us. I've heard it said that we should view Revelation as a picture book, not a puzzle book. See it in broad strokes, and don't get bogged down in every detail that you might not fully understand.

I'll be the first to admit, I don't understand every single verse in the book. But I understand enough of it to know something very important. We win! As we come to the end of this book, I hope that has been a source of encouragement to you. Let's close out the book. Look at Revelation 22:18-21:

I warn everyone who hears the words of the prophecy of this book: if anyone adds to them, God will add to him the plagues described in this book, and if anyone takes away from the words of the book of this prophecy, God will take away his share in the tree of life and in the holy city, which are described in this book. He who testifies to these things says, "Surely I am coming soon." Amen. Come, Lord Jesus! The grace of the Lord Jesus be with all. Amen.

These verses teach us not to add or take away from the prophecies in the book. This means to have a balanced and Biblical approach to Revelation. I hope I have achieved that. We shouldn't speculate beyond what it says, and we shouldn't ignore what it says. May the words in this book be a source of great comfort to us. May it cause us to have a deeper craving for Christ and a yearning for glory. May it fuel us to reach others with the gospel. Come, Lord Jesus!

Closing Benediction: "May we be greatly comforted by Your words to us, Jesus. May we leave this book with a greater craving for Your presence, Heavenly Father. Amen."

Notes

1. "St. Patrick's Breastplate," Blue Letter Bible, n.d., https://www.blueletterbible.org/hymns/s/St_Patricks_Breastplate.cfm.

2. Rice, Wayne. *Hot Illustrations for Youth Talks*. Zondervan, 1993.

3. Phillips, John. *Exploring Romans: An Expository Commentary*. Kregel Academic & Professional, 2002.

4. Lawrence, John. Down to Earth: The laws of the Harvest. Multnomah Press; Edition Unstated (January 1, 1975).

5. Charles R. Swindoll Quotes. BrainyQuote.com, BrainyMedia Inc, 2024. https://www.brainyquote.com/quotes/charles_r_swindoll_578721, accessed July 29, 2024.

6. "30 Best Vance Havner Quotes With Image," Bookey, September 14, 2023, https://www.bookey.app/quote-author/vance-havner#:~:text=Vance%20Havner's%20quote,%20%22A%20faith,challenges%20in%20one's%20spiritual%20journey.

7. Tozer, A.W. *The Knowledge of the Holy*. HarperOne; 31935th edition (October 6, 2009).

8. Mark Twain Quotes. BrainyQuote.com. BrainyMedia Inc, 2024, https://www.brainyquote.com/quotes/mark_twain_103756.

9. Spurgeon, Charles. *The Complete Works of C. H. Spurgeon, Volume 32: Sermons 1877-1937*. Delmarva Publications, 2013.

10. Environment America Research & Policy Center. "Trash in America," Environement America Research and Policy Center, September 29, 2021, https://environmentamerica.org/center/resources/trash-in-america-2/#:~:text=The%20U.S.%20produces%20more%20than,such%20as%20universities%20and%20libraries.

11. Newell, William. *Revelation: A Complete Commentary*. World Pub, 1987.

12. Hewitt, E. (1898). When We All Get To Heaven. https://hymnary.org/text sing_the_wondrous_love_of_jesus_sing_his

13. Rice, Grantland. "The Four Horsemen." New York Herald Tribune. October 18, 1924.

14. "Preaching Boldly | Ministry127," n.d., https://ministry127.com/resources/illustration/preaching-boldly.

15. Swindoll, Charles. *Insights on Revelation (Swindoll's Living Insights New Testament Commentary)*. Tyndale House Publishers, 2014.

16. Watts, Isaac. "There Is A Land Of Pure Delight,"1709, https://hymnary.org/text/there_is_a_land_of_pure_delight_where_sa.

17. "Has Everyone Heard." Joshua Project, accessed January 2, 2025, https://joshuaproject.net/resources/articles/has_everyone_heard.

18. Palau, Luis. *Experiencing God's Forgiveness: Being Freed from Sin and Guilt.* Multnomah Books, 1984.

19. Bounds, E.M. Rice, *Power Through Prayer.* Rough Draft Printing, 2013.

20. Anthelme Brillat-Savarin, Jean. *The Physiology of Taste.* Vintage; Reprint edition (October 4, 2011).

21. "Preaching Boldly." Ministry127," n.d. accessed January 2, 2025, https://ministry127.com/resources/illustration/preaching-boldly.

22. A.W. Tozer, quoted in D.J. Fant. A.W. Tozer, Christian Publications, 1964.

23. Papke, David R. "Karl Marx on Religion – Marquette University Law School Faculty Blog," January 20, 2015, https://law.marquette.edu/facultyblog/2015/01/karl-marx-on-religion/comment-page-1/#:~:text=My%20best%20translation%20of%20those,rather%20as%20a%20secular%20humanist.

24. Alcorn, Randy. *Heaven.* Tyndale Momentum, 2004.

25. Greenwalt, Julie. "When Barry Bremen Tried to Infiltrate the Dallas Cowgirls, the Team Found It a Drag," *People,* vol. 13, no. 2 (Jan. 14, 1980).

26. Frost, Robert, et al. The Road Not Taken: A Selection of Robert Frost's Poems. New York, H. Holt and Co, 1991.

27. Spurgeon, Charles. *Spurgeon at His Best.* Baker Book House, 1988.

28. Leake, Mike. "The Backstory To Spurgeon's 'If Sinners Be Damned…'" Borrowed Light. https://www.mikeleake.net/2023/08/the-backstory-to-spurgeons-if-sinners-be-damned.html

29. Lucado, Max. *Come Thirsty: No Heart Too Dry for His Touch.* Thomas Nelson; Reprint edition (April 30, 2012)

30. "Glory Is Forever." Illustration Exchange. https://illustrationexchange.com/illustrations?category=464

Tony Tice

Tony is husband to his beautiful bride Becky, dad to six incredible kids, and a grandpa. Tony has served as a pastor for over three decades, ministering in churches of all sizes. He presently serves as the lead pastor of a new church in northern Indiana, Church on the Rock. Tony has traveled around the world teaching God's Word. He has published numerous books, Bible studies, and devotionals. Tony's mission is to help people fall in love with the Word of God so that they will fall more in love with the God of the Word.

www.ingramcontent.com/pod-product-compliance
Lightning Source LLC
Chambersburg PA
CBHW070129080526
44586CB00015B/1619